# GET

# HOUSED

The Definitive Guide
to Making Housing Law Work
For You.

Lynden Swift

GREEN YAFFLE PRESS

Green Yaffle Press

www.greenyafflepress.com

info@greenyafflepress.co.uk

978-0-9575829-3-4

© Green Yaffle Press

Edition 1.2

2016

# Contents

# Introduction

This book is designed to give you the information and tools you need to get either yourself (or if you are a professional adviser, a client), housed as quickly and directly as possible by making use of the statutory safety net which is available to anyone in housing need.

This is, above all, a practical book. We begin with a quick overview of how homelessness works, what it requires your local council to look at and what duties it imposes on them. This forms the basis for all the challenges you will be shown in this book.

We then look at each of these challenges that you can throw at your local council's housing department, to get you or your client housed. We then look at how a local council might defend itself against these and how to get around any potential arguments. We also look at a number of other legal duties outside of homeless legislation that you can also use to help secure accommodation and assistance for someone in housing need.

By the end of the book you will have three new abilities:

- Know what a local authority's duties are towards anyone in housing need.

- Know how to require a local authority to carry out those duties.

- Know how to challenge a homelessness decision after a local authority has carried out those duties.

The end result: you (or your client) will know exactly how to get yourself housed.

This book focuses on how to challenge English local authority homeless decisions (though many of the principles can also be applied to Welsh and Scottish authorities). It is not a guide to homelessness legislation per se. It is recommended that you use some of the recommended books or websites listed in the resources section for background information for when you need more information on case law, legislation and procedures.

Alongside this book are cloud files you can download. These add extra information which might be useful, especially to advice agencies. They are available to download from the following links

https://app.box.com/GetHousedDocuments

Because this book is designed to help both advice agencies and individuals trying to help themselves, I will sometimes refer to 'you' and sometimes to 'your client'. Take these as interchangeable.

Where any 'sections' are referred to, this means sections of Part 7 of the 1996 Homelessness Act. In the reference section at the end are listed sources of more in-depth information on the many pieces of legislation and case law surrounding housing and homelessness.

# 1. Gatekeeping and the Prevention of Homelessness Applications

Imagine that you have 10 houses to give away. Outside your door is a crowd of 100 people. How do you decide which 10 get housed? This is the difficult dynamic faced by every local council homelessness department everyday. To guide their hand in this decision making there exists both statutory legislation and case law. The problem is that both of these seem to have become sidelined as guiding principles when people approach their local council and seek help with their housing.

Working in a number of local authority homeless departments I have seen the effects of the government's 'prevention of homelessness' agenda at first hand. My experience is that it has forced local councils to neglect their legal duties to people in housing need in order to ensure that government targets are met. As a result, people in housing need seeking help are being denied their full legal rights to which they are entitled. It is my belief that this is wrong.

How the system should work is this. If you or I approach our local homeless department and ask for help, the law places a duty on the council to firstly quickly assesses whether our approach gives them a reason to believe (not proof), that we might be homeless or threatened with homelessness within the next 28 days. That simple test which has a very low threshold of acceptance is the sole trigger for the entire statutory process of a homelessness application.

If the council also has a reason to believe that we might be eligible for public funds, might be homeless and might have a priority need, then we should also be provided with accommodation.

This second test should be concluded on the same day that we approach and ask for help, so that we are not left on the streets that night. It too has a low threshold of acceptance so that if there is any doubt, the council should provide some accommodation for us whilst it investigates further.

At the end of the process (which involves a more thorough investigation), we receive a formal decision letter setting out the council's decision, what evidence it is based on and how that evidence has led to the decision. This is what a homelessness application entails and it is every person's legal right when faced with homelessness. Except, that's not exactly how it has worked out over the past decade under the government's 'prevention agenda'

Prior to 2002, if you went to see your local council's homelessness department because you were either homeless or potentially homeless, the above scenario is pretty much what would have happened. Then, in 2002, the government department for homelessness (Communities and Local Government), came up with the idea of local councils doing more to 'prevent homelessness'. What this meant in theory (and to be fair, often in practice), was that your local council was to become more proactive in taking steps to either prevent you from losing your current accommodation or, if that was not possible, to actively find you somewhere else or at the very least, help you to do so. Who could argue with such a positive sounding initiative?

On one level it seemed to work. Officially the number of people recorded as homeless plummeted, decreasing year on year. The number of rough sleepers dropped to as close to zero as had ever been seen. The government patted itself on the back. Local councils throughout the land even renamed the job titles of their Homelessness Officers to 'Advice Officers' or 'Prevention Officers' because, well, no one was really homeless any more were they?

What this meant in practice however (in my experience) and what really went down year on year, was the number of formal homelessness applications being taken and recorded. In the drive for prevention, councils were unofficially (but strongly) discouraged from recording anyone's approach as a formal Homelessness Application unless it was absolutely inescapable; much to the frustration of staff in housing and support organisations representing homeless people across England.

What this has led to is that instead of assessing each person who asks for help according to the law, i.e. by carrying out a formal investigation and giving each individual or family an official decision letter at the end of the process, 'Prevention Officers' often carry out only a quick face to face assessment and make their (often verbal) decisions there and then.

If an applicant seems likely to have a priority need (such as dependent children), then they are often offered a loan for a deposit and rent in advance on a private tenancy. If the applicant manages to find somewhere then this is duly recorded as a 'prevention'. But not as a homelessness application.

If the prevention officer believes that the council might not have any legal duty then the person might only be given some general 'advice' on housing and sent on their way. Such an approach is not required to be recorded at all and certainly not as a homelessness application (though a local council might itself choose to record it as an 'advice only' approach, just for it's own records). Either way, not so much as a legal decision in site.

Without any formal homelessness application being taken, a person is absolutely denied their statutory rights to apply for housing, denied their potential offer of social housing and denied their legal right to appeal any negative decision (because no official decision is ever made).

In many homelessness departments, I perceive this same approach still in operation today. All of which is a shame, because there is no inherent conflict between actually preventing a person's homelessness if possible whilst still taking and investigating a legal homelessness application. The conflict comes when the latter is what is measured and becomes a target to be met. Then people's rights suffer in the drive to ensure that official figures come within that government target and that target takes priority over a council's legal duties and people's real need.

One of the most serious effects of the government's prevention programme is that we as a nation now have no idea of the real level of housing need in this country because of the way in which the government requires local authorities to record and measure homelessness.

Local councils are required to record the demand for their homeless services in two broad ways: by the number of statutory homelessness applications they open and by the number of 'prevention applications' they open. The official homelessness level is measured only by the first figure.

There are two significant problems with this. The first is that so called 'prevention applications' have no real existence in law and legally, most should probably be recorded as homelessness applications but they are not and so they are not counted in the official statistics for homelessness. The second is that if combined with a general 'gate-keeping' approach, this measure also excludes the number of people who approach their local council and ask for help but who do not have either a homelessness or a prevention case recorded but are simply dealt with as an 'advice only' case: a legally meaningless and non-existent type of application. The figures of homeless applications and approaches should map each other fairly closely. Instead, where the latter is known at all, they are wildly disparate.

The effect of this is that the true level of housing need in this country is now not known at all at a national level; a shocking state of national ignorance. Prior to 2002, the number of homelessness applications did act as a fairly accurate indicator of the level of demand of housing need. Now, it is a measure only of those few who managed to get through all of the obstacles and have a formal homelessness application taken. The real figure of need is the total number of people approaching their local council asking for help with their housing. Whilst some local authorities will record this for internal purposes, there is no national level recording of this and so the degree of need across the country is unknown.

It is difficult to prove that any particular local authority is not dealing with homeless approaches in the way that they legally should, but a number of studies have reached similar concerns about the effect of the government's prevention agenda on how local authorities deliver homelessness services. Here are just two examples:

Local Authority Homelessness Prevention in England: Empowering Consumers or Denying Rights, by Hal Pawson.

Homelessness: The Challenge of Prevention. *http://bit.ly/1EmclC8*

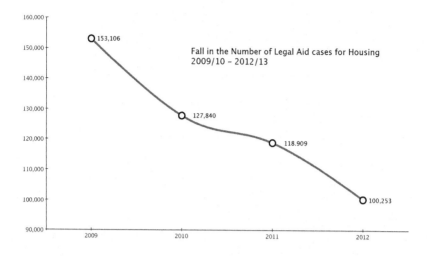

*Figure 1: The fall in the number of legal aid cases for housing.*
*Source: LAG Report on the decline in availability of Legal Aid.*

If you carry out a web search on 'homelessness gate-keeping' you will find many other sources of concern.

Since 2010 the situation has been worsened by cuts to legal aid resulting in a significant drop in both the number of people able to find support and the number of legal representatives willing to provide this assistance.

The report detailing the effect of the cuts to legal aid, produced by the Legal Action Group can be found at:

*http://www.lag.org.uk/policy-campaigns/legal-aid-secret-service.aspx*
or, for a shorter link: *http://bit.ly/1aPiR9H*

This has taken place in a wider context of welfare cuts, economic downturn and a continual rise in the cost of rented accommodation. The need for the statutory safety net is thus arguably greater today than ever before.

Why does all of this matter? It matters because if you approach your local council for help with your housing, you will only have access to your full legal rights if you have a homelessness application taken. Without it, you have nothing. Without it, your request for help doesn't even officially exist.

Part of the reason for this book is the simple sharing of knowledge. I have seen organisations representing vulnerable clients fail time and time again to get their clients housed because they did not know how the law for homelessness worked nor the right buttons to press to get action. Similarly, I have seen individuals continually fail to receive the full help to which they are entitled, because of the way local councils have been forced to deal with such approaches.

This book will show you what should happen when you approach your local council and ask for help with your housing. It will explain each of the tests which a local council should apply and explain how to show that you (or your clients) meet these tests. It will also show you what to do if a council doesn't seem to be remembering its legal duties and how you can remind them. The end result is that armed with this knowledge of your legal rights to be housed; you're more likely to be.

# 2. Homelessness or Prevention

First of all; a bit of myth busting. There is no such thing as a homelessness application. At least not in any material sense. It's not a form. It's not type of interview. It's not a 'thing'. It's just a set of conditions. What makes a homelessness application a homelessness application is a person going to their local council and giving them reason to believe that the person might be homeless or threatened with homelessness in the next 28 days. That's it. The local authority doesn't have any say in this; its duties are triggered automatically whenever these conditions occur.

Although the statutory duty exists, strange to say, you might not always wish to make use of it. Homelessness departments can be viewed as having two distinct sides; the Prevention side and the Statutory side. The former is often informal, helpful and flexible. The latter can be strict and sometimes not in a household's best interest. Use your own discretion to decide which is best for you or your client.

'Prevention departments' can access a wide range of tools and funds which can be used to either prevent someone from losing their accommodation or enable access to alternative accommodation.

Such tools include mediation, payments towards arrears, assistance with access to discretionary housing payments, financial assistance with rent in advance, deposits, moving costs and agency fees. The limits are often defined by what someone actually asks for; if a solution would prevent homelessness, most local authority prevention departments would be willing to try to make it work.

The statutory assessment on the other hand is designed as a process to facilitate the allocation of a scarce resource. It is designed to 'weed' people out so that only the most 'needy' remain. Sometimes it is the most appropriate solution, but not always.

The following points are to be a guide. Discuss the options with your client and mutually decide on the best course of action.

## When to push for a homelessness application

- To get a client housed. You are satisfied that there is a clear duty and you want to see it fulfilled.

- To get a client help if you believe that they are not being given the full range of statutory assistance. This might be the case if the prevention option has not really worked. It also enables every action of the local authority to be accountable and challengeable, including offers of temporary accommodation and any discharges of duty.

- To receive a decision letter which can be challenged. This is the main reason and is very important.

- If it is an emergency and your client will be homeless otherwise. This gives you access to the s188 duty of interim accommodation and gives you time to gather information whilst your client is housed.


## When to not push for a homelessness application

- You have a good relationship with your local authority housing department. You may be confident that your particular housing department assess all presentations properly and gives each one the best possible solution. It is probably true that pushing for a statutory homelessness assessment for every client, even though it is the law, is likely to put a strain on your relationship with your colleagues in the local authority and this is something which may have to be dealt with between respective managers.

- Temporary Accommodation would not be suitable. Being placed into a bed and breakfast type establishment may not be the most appropriate option for your client. Whilst you can challenge the suitability of any accommodation offered, many types of supported accommodation are available which are accessible through 'prevention' routes without needing a statutory homelessness assessment. This might be a more suitable option.

- Intentionality. If you believe that this is a risk, then you need to be sure that you can successfully defend any such decision and overturn it. If not, it may be best to avoid the homelessness route and seek solutions through the prevention options available.
- Private Rented Sector Options (PRSO). If your local authority operates such a scheme then your only route of challenge is on the basis of the suitability of accommodation offered. This significantly narrows your range of options for challenge as all of the statutory tests will have been accepted in order to make a PRSO offer.

Surprise your local authority. Homelessness departments are staffed by people who work under great pressure in terms of client numbers, financial constraints and government pressures. Most of the time they genuinely care and want to help people. Like any organisation, they work best when approached in ways that make things easy for them. Approach and say you would like to make a 'Prevention Application'. After the raised eyebrows, you might be surprised at the service you receive.

# 3. An Overview: How Homelessness Works

If you believe that a statutory homelessness application is needed you can go to your local council and ask for help. What should happen is that if your local authority has reason to believe that you are eligible for public funds and might be homeless within 28 days then its statutory duties are triggered. It must begin investigating your situation according to the 'five tests' and it must carry out its duties according to how they are set out in the four main duties and its powers. If you are homeless on the day you approach your council then they must accommodate you if you might have what is called a 'priority need'. At the end of the process you must be given an official decision letter which must set out the reasoning behind the decision.

It is a rather antiquated process and it is designed to winnow out those to whom the local authority has a duty towards and those it does not and can legally leave on the street. The good news though is that pretty much every bit of the process is open to challenge and challenging each part is actually pretty easy. The bulk of it does not involve court action nor legal advisors; people can easily be in charge of challenging their own housing decisions to get themselves housed. Voluntary organisations such as Citizens Advice Bureau or Shelter or others can also help many of their clients into housing without needing to pay for professional legal assistance for the bulk of the process, though of course they will have their own time and staff constraints. Currently though, because they typically do not use a lot of the challenges set out in this guide, all third sector organisations can improve their 'success rate' massively, in terms of the number of clients they are able to get housed.

Let's have a look at what these 'tests and duties' are.

## The Five Tests

When you approach your local council and ask for assistance with your housing need, they are required to carry out five specific tests in order to decide what duties they have towards you. Each of these carries its own subset of tests, legal definitions and case law clarifications. Each is an area on which you can focus a challenge.

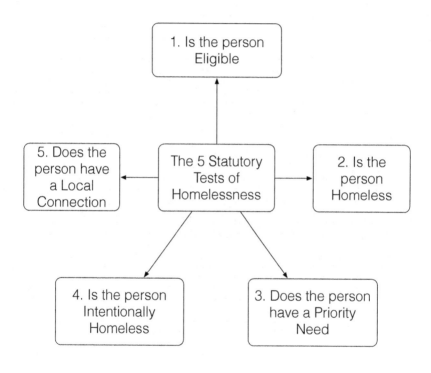

*Figure 2: The five tests of homelessness.*

## The Five Duties

Alongside the 5 tests, there are 5 duties which a local authority must carry out, including 1 power which it has a duty to consider using (hence its inclusion here). Each of these is also an area on which you can focus a challenge.

We will look at all of these, and ways around them, in more detail later.

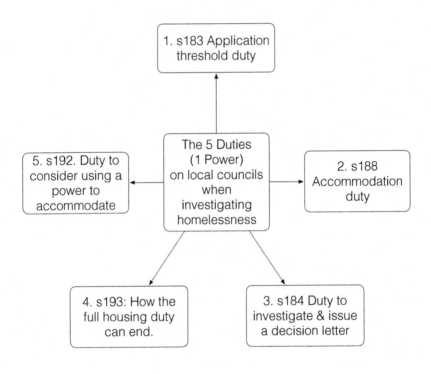

*Figure 3: The five duties.*

## Key Concept: 'Person'

Literature on homelessness legislation tends to use the terms 'person', 'applicant' and 'household' slightly interchangeably. In legal terms, there is only one actual applicant per application. However, the duties owed to that applicant must take into consideration their applicability to anyone who resides with the applicant or who may reasonably be expected to reside.

This is a very important concept to keep in mind as it can be used to challenge and render void a number of legal tests which might, on the face of it, exclude your client. We will return to this throughout this guide.

Use the criteria for each of these tests to structure either your initial submissions of support pre s184 decision or your challenges to a s202 review. Look for evidence that the local authority has used them to structure their investigations and has included them in their decision letter.

# 4. The Initial Duties

In this section, we're going to set out the initial triggers to getting a homeless application taken. Understanding and applying these essential triggers are the key to ensuring that the rest of the process takes place.

## The Application Threshold

s183: If a local authority have reason to believe a person might be homeless or threatened with homelessness within 28 days.

Making a homelessness application is, in theory, very simple. When a person approaches a local authority and the above applies then the statutory duties are triggered.

The manner of approach is not defined in law and can be made in person, by phone, by email or letter and by a third party on behalf of the person.

No proofs are required. Only a 'reason to believe'. The threshold is deliberately set very low. It simply means that you have given your council a 'reason to believe' that you might be homeless.

## The Accommodation Threshold

s188: Where a local authority has reason to believe a person might be homeless and might be eligible and might have a priority need.

Where s183 has been triggered, if the local authority have a 'reason to believe' that the person might be homeless that night, then they must provide that person with accommodation.

The threshold is again low; it does not require that the applicant provide the local authority with proof that they are homeless, eligible or in 'priority need' - only that they might be.

Accommodation is to be provided whilst the authority carry out their investigations and reach a decision.

## Re-Applications

This has always been a rather unclear area of housing law and still is.

The OLD test was that there must have been a 'material change of circumstances' If you receive such a decision from a local authority then that decision is immediately challengeable on Administrative Law grounds because the local authority has applied the wrong test. Look for this because its a very common mistake.

The NEW test is whether a re-application is being made on exactly the same circumstances. It is a much lower threshold.

A local authority can only refuse to take a new application if any change of facts are 'fanciful or trivial'. The case law is unclear on exactly what this means and it is for the applicant to identify such changes.

In reality this is usually of little real benefit unless you know of changes that render a previous decision void. Whilst circumstances may have changed to allow a new application, if the local authority can simply issue an identical decision, the client benefit is low.

The exception might be on a decision of Intentionality, where, even if the decision is the same, your client would be owed another period of accommodation whilst they found somewhere more permanent to live. Though this is usually taken to be 28 days, it's actually whatever is reasonable for your client. And this is challengeable. So it might be worth applying for a re-application on this ground alone and if a new decision of intentionality is issued, applying for a s202 review on the grounds that 28 days is not reasonable. We will look at this in more detail later on.

# 5. How to Challenge the Initial Duties

## Judicial Review

The homelessness process has three types of challenge; Judicial Review, s202 Reviews and s204 Appeals. Judicial Reviews tackle those actions of a local authority which are not included in the s202 or s204 processes and focus on situations where you believe that the local authority is not carrying out its public duties properly and where there is no other right of appeal.

The challenge to any of the three duties we have just covered is, in theory, by an application for a Judicial Review of the local authority's decision (to not accept an application or provide accommodation for example).

In practice, a full judicial review hearing should almost never be necessary; the local authority will back down long before then due to the excessive cost and the fact that it knows it wont win.

The following is really for the benefit of advice organisations. If you are a person seeking housing; get such an organisation on your side to do this bit for you.

The way to use the potential for a Judicial Review of such decisions is this:

1. Submit an informal letter to the manager of the housing department stating your request (for Mr X to be provided with accommodation pending a decision or for a formal homelessness application to be taken for Mrs Y, etc.) and your intention of applying for a judicial review if your request is not complied with.

Be sure to include a paragraph stating that you would rather avoid a costly legal process concerning this matter where the threshold is very low and that you hope that this request can be resolved informally. In many instances, this will be all that is required.

2. If not, the next stage is to submit a more formal pre-action protocol letter, giving a defined time-frame for the local authority to comply with your request to avoid you formally

making an application to the court for a Judicial Review hearing and an emergency injunction (to force the local authority to do what you are asking them to do; i.e. take an application or provide interim accommodation).

3. It is unlikely that a typical local authority will resist this. However, if it does then you must proceed with the judicial review process either yourself by following the guidance and forms as set out in the following two links or by engaging the assistance of a local legal professional.

Pre-Action Protocol for Judicial Review: *http://www.justice.gov.uk/ courts/procedure-rules/civil/protocol/prot_jrv*

Bitly: *http://bit.ly/1egksGi*

Legal forms and guidance: *http://www.justice.gov.uk/downloads/ courts/administrative-court/applying-for-judicial-review.pdf*

Bitly: *http://bit.ly/1i3LAqn*

I would recommend a mixture of the two. The process of judicial review for homelessness applications can be expensive and is always very time consuming. It is also complicated and has to be carried out in exactly the right way, in terms of form completion and court submissions and it is easy to get it wrong if you don't know what you are doing or just haven't done it before.

Because it is so useful however, it is something which is really worth learning and if you can get a local legal advice specialist to show you how to go about it, then that will make any subsequent applications you have to make much easier. Probably the most effective way is for you to handle as much of the paperwork and interviewing of a client as possible with your local legal representatives assisting with the submission of court papers.

Judicial Review is expensive and the number of legal aid practitioners has, in effect, fallen off a cliff, but there is a very good reason why it is worth meeting the cost of a full judicial review application. You will, in all likelihood, only have to do it the once.

# The Value of Learning the Judicial Review Process.

A local authority knows that it doesn't have a leg to stand on if it tries to defend not taking a homeless application or not accommodating a household under these initial duties. It knows that any application for judicial review is simply not worth while defending because it would cost the local authority far more in legal fees than it would in accommodation costs. But it needs to know that you mean it when you say you will apply for a judicial review if they do not act. Therefore, you might have to invest the money and time in pursuing a judicial review for real the first time. In all likelihood, it will end up being the last time.

In reality, once you make the application for an emergency injunction, the local authority will capitulate before any actual hearing takes place - to save on costs. On subsequent occasions, you probably wont even need to go that far and the initial informal letter requesting action should be all that is required.

Getting this right will win you future success in gaining accommodation. It is something which is worth investing time and money in to do it properly. Once your local authority knows you will carry through threats of Judicial Review, they are much more likely to back down on subsequent occasions. They simply cannot afford to fight every single JR application which falls on their desk. The easiest way they can avoid this is to simply carry out the duties the law requires of them.

Next we will look at the five tests of homelessness and how to use each one of them to help get a person housed.

# 6. The Main Duties: The Five Tests of Homeless Law

Now that we have looked at the initial duties around ensuring that an application is taken and accommodation is provided, we move on to the main body of investigations and tests that a homeless department carries out in order to reach a decision on a person's case.

When your local authority investigates a homelessness application, it is required to examine whether the person of household is eligible for housing assistance, homeless, in priority need and homeless intentionally or not. A local authority is not required to consider local connection, but invariably will and will often consider it first. These are the ones shown in Figure 2 above and the trigger the duties shown in Figure 3 above.

We will look at each of these areas in turn, examining what the tests require a local authority to consider, ways to show how a person fits the requirements and how to challenge each area if a local authority decides that a person's application fails at any particular stage.

# 7. Eligibility (and how to be eligible)

Immigration is an area of law which a) gets very complicated very quickly and b) is subject to revisions and updates from both statutory and case law with alarming frequency and regularity.

We are going to concentrate on the most common area seen in practice; that of the rights to housing of European (EEA) Nationals.

## Quick and simple guide to EEA eligibility

EEA Nationals are not subject to immigration control and so, on the face of it, are eligible for housing assistance. But: prescribed exceptions do apply. Almost everything about EEA eligibility revolves around whether or not the person is a worker. This is where you will likely focus your challenge to any negative eligibility decision for an EEA National. A very simple overview is given in Figures 4 & 5. If an EEA National is not currently working, their eligibility will depend on:

1. Whether any family members are eligible.

2. Whether they still have worker status from any previous work.

3. Whether they have eligibility for any other reason such as length of residence.

If an EEA National has previously worked, you will have to look at the circumstances around how and why that work ended and what the person has done since. Figures 6 & 7 show these conditions but they revolve around whether the work ended voluntarily and whether the person is on any work related training and is registered as a job seeker. It is suggested that a person retains 'worker status' for 6 months. This is not set in stone but is a useful working threshold; if a person has been out of work for longer than 6 months, you will likely find it more difficult to demonstrate eligibility for housing assistance as a 'work seeker'. Not impossible, but more difficult.

One important concept to remember (to avoid confusion), is that we are talking here specifically about eligibility for housing assistance. A person can be eligible for public funds and able to claim benefits but still not be eligible for housing assistance. Don't use one to argue for the other; eligibility for housing assistance is specific and really revolves around worker status.

Use the flowcharts in figures 6 & 7 to help you to assess the eligibility of an EEA National who is not currently working.

## Challenging EEA Eligibility Decisions

The three simplest ways to overcome any negative decision on eligibility for an EEA National are to show how that person is either a worker, self employed or is a family member of someone who is. Let's look at each of these in turn.

**1. As A Worker**

Confusingly, an EEA National can be eligible for income benefits, such as Job Seekers Allowance (JSA) and Housing Benefits, but not be eligible for housing assistance. The legislation is drafted to focus eligibility on people classified as 'workers' or family members of such. Therefore, in order for an EEA national to be eligible for housing assistance, they need to be able to show that they fall within this test.

A worker is defined by three factors:

1. The person must perform services of an economic value which must not be on such a small scale as to be 'marginal or ancillary' (i.e. often ancillary to the main reason for being in the UK, e.g. this would not render a student eligible).

2. The work must be for services for and under the direction of another. Many temporary workers are caught by this because their contracts state that they have a 'contract OF service' rather than a 'contract FOR services', with 'no obligation on the part of the agency to offer work or of the contractor to accept any work offered'.

3. The person must receive remuneration. It does not matter that any such remuneration is so small that they must also claim benefits.

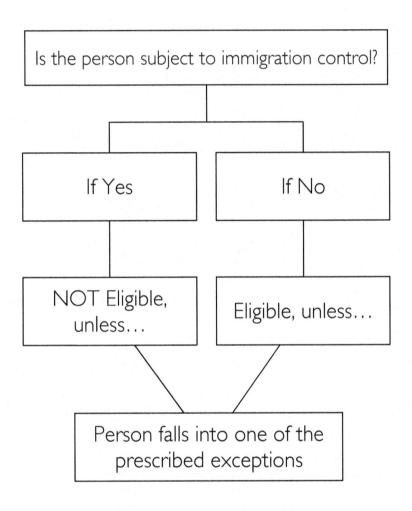

Figure 4: How immigration law works.

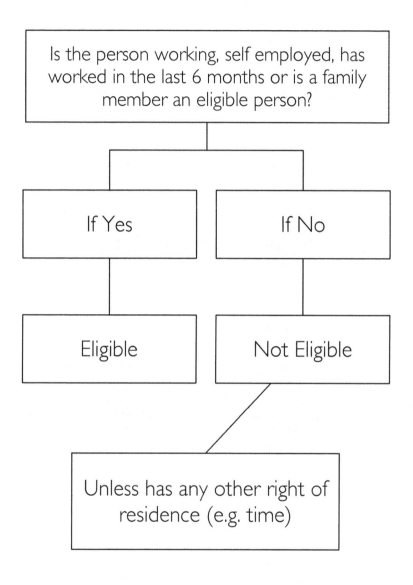

*Figure 5: Overview of EEA Eligibility & Worker Status.*

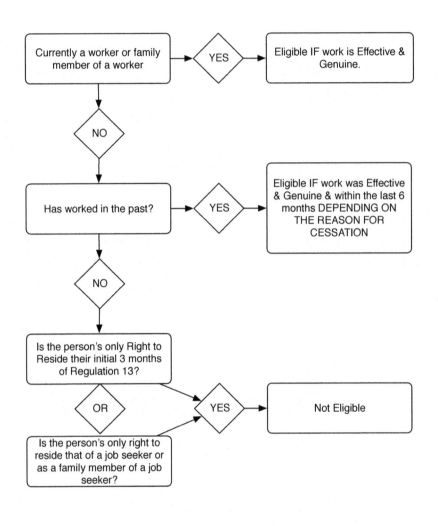

Figure 6: How to check an EEA National's Eligibility if not currently working.

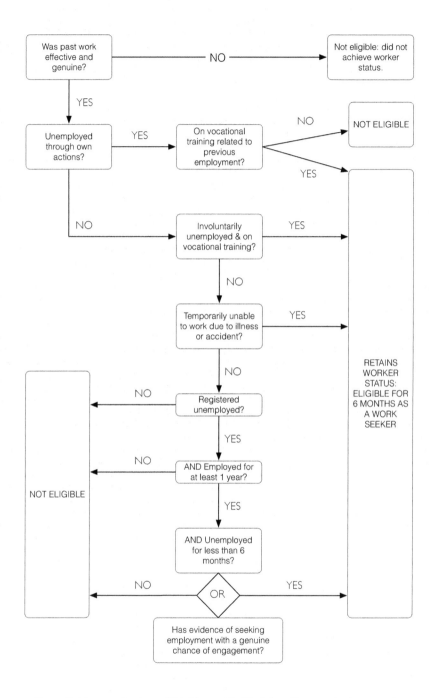

*Figure 7: How to check an EEA National's Eligibility if has worked previously.*

If your client has been found to be ineligible due to not being a worker, the simplest challenge is to take up a part time job. Just two hours a day is sufficient to bring them within the definition of a worker.

If a person ceases employment, refer to Figures 6 & 7 to check if they retain their status as a worker. A person who is claiming unemployment benefits may still have 'worker' status in eligibility terms, despite what their benefit status might imply.

It is also worth noting that simply being on unemployment benefits will often be enough for a person to be accepted as eligible by a local authority; even though they may not actually be eligible for housing assistance. It's something which local authorities commonly get wrong due to the complex and confusing nature of this area of law.

## 2. As Self Employed. (Sell the Big Issue).

Being self employed is currently the simplest way for any EEA national to gain full eligibility for housing assistance and it can be as straightforward as simply selling the Big Issue magazine.

In Bristol in 2011 an Upper Tribunal court found that a Romanian Big Issue seller was self employed and therefore eligible under the regulations for housing assistance as a self employed person.

Whilst not binding on other authorities, Bristol Council could find no grounds of law on which to appeal this case and so therefore, neither will any other local authority when faced with a similar case.

Each situation will be different and will turn on its merits so look for similarities between this case and your client's.

You can view the legal documents here: *https://www.bristol.gov. uk/committee/2012/ta/ta000/0327_11c.pdf*

Bitly: *http://bit.ly/1fMDEZ5*

You can view the Big Issue's own guidance to sellers here:

*http://equality.uk.com/The_Big_Issue_files/Factsheet%20Self-employment%20and%20working%20with%20The%20Big%20Issue. pdf*

Bitly: *http://bit.ly/1diQ8ED*

Use this to justify how your client is self employed as a big issue seller. This really is the easiest way to gain eligibility and its unlikely that this loophole will be closed any time soon.

## General Issues on Self Employment.

The Big Issue case aside, for a person to be considered eligible as a self employed person, the most important point is that they demonstrate a 'Genuine Business Presence'. This simply means that it should be readily obvious that the person is self employed.

Things which will help a person to demonstrate this are:

• Registering with HMRC as self employed.

• Have business cards.

• Have a website.

• Be able to produce accounts.

• Have an accountant.

It is also clear from the courts that a self employed person cannot be expected to be in 'work' continuously; there will be periods when there will be no work; that is the nature of self employment. Such a person does not lose their eligibility during those periods. All of which makes setting up a business, however small the income and however infrequent the work, probably the fastest and easiest way for an EEA national to come within the eligibility criteria.

## 3. As A Family Member of an Eligible Person

Family members has a specific meaning in this context. It means a Married Spouse, a Registered Civil Partner, a dependent child under 21 and a dependent or direct ascending relative; i.e. a parent.

If an applicant has a family member who is eligible for any reason whatsoever, then they are considered to be eligible due to the status of their family member.

# 8. Homelessness

Whether or not you are considered to be homeless is the second test that your local homelessness department will apply. It's not simple test and many people who might consider themselves as homeless will not be considered so by their local council. Likewise, you might be in a situation where you think that you are not eligible for any help but actually would be considered to be legally homeless.

The legal definition is found in sections 175-177 of the 1996 Housing Act, Part 7. In essence, you are considered to be homeless if, now or within the next 28 days, you (or anyone you reside with or might reasonably be expected to reside with), have no accommodation available to which you have any kind of legal right to stay in or, if you do have somewhere to stay, if that accommodation is not available, not reasonable to occupy, you cannot secure entry to it or, if it is a moveable structure (such as a boat or a motor-home), you have nowhere you can legally place it to reside in. What these sections amount to in practice is a test which has seven distinct elements, with some having their own sub-tests. Figure 8 shows the seven 'arms' of how the test of homelessness is constructed.

Each of these tests, and their sub-tests, are areas for you to gather evidence demonstrating how you fit the criteria or against which you can launch a challenge if the local authority decides you don't. A person has to not 'fit' just one of these tests or conditions to be considered homeless. Always remember that 'person' means the applicant, anyone they reside with and anyone they may reasonably be expected to reside with. The homeless test also includes if any of the criteria are likely to apply to anyone in the household in the next 28 days. So if any person within that group can say 'no' to any of these seven tests or their sub tests, or might be able to in the next 28 days, then all are statutorily homeless. Make use of this.

Some of these tests are more suitable for using as a basis for showing homelessness than others. While we will take a look at all seven, some are fairly easily dealt with due to their relative straightforwardness while others we will delve into a bit more deeply because they contain a rich seam of grounds on which to

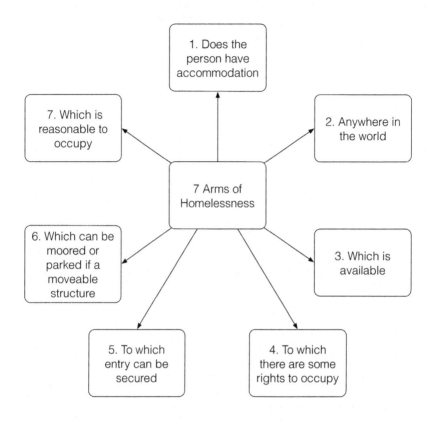

*Figure 8: The 7 point test of Homelessness.*

mount a case for a successful homeless decision.

Figure 9 gives an overview and flow-through of the tests and the process which every homelessness officer will (or should) follow when investigating your situation to assess whether you are homeless or not.

The next section looks at what these tests involve, what your homeless officer will look at when interviewing you or investigating your application and how to use these tests to get accepted at initial decision level or to challenge a negative decision at review level.

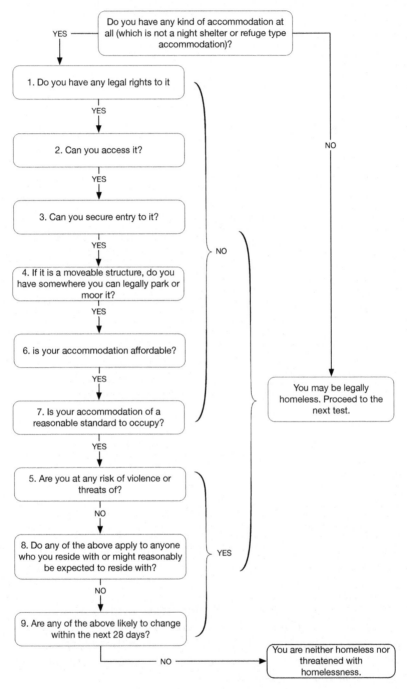

Figure 9: How the test of Homelessness is applied

# The 7-Point Test of Homelessness

## 1. Do you have accommodation?

This is rarely a ground for challenging a homeless decision because it is rarely an area of dispute. It is accepted by homeless departments that night shelters, refuges, prisons and hospitals are not to be considered as accommodation.

The one exception has been women's refuges where it has been held that where residents have been given self contained, longer term tenancies; what are in effect AST's, then they might not be considered homeless. This is a less usual situation however as such residents are not likely to be applying as homeless from such accommodation. If they do, their assessment is normally affected one way or another by one of the remaining tests.

## 2. Anywhere in the world?

Local authorities are entitled to take into consideration any accommodation to which the application might have access, regardless of where in the world it might be. Should they find out that a household has accommodation somewhere else in the world, it is open to them to consider that person 'not homeless'. The ways around such a decision are to argue that the person is homeless because the accommodation fails one of the other criteria below.

## 3. Which is available?

Available means available for occupation by the applicant, anyone they reside with or may reasonably be expected to reside with.

This is often the most effective one to use where family members are concerned. Look for reasons why the accommodation is not suitable applying all of the homeless criteria to each and every person in the applicant's household. Just one ground has to apply to just one person for the entire household to be statutorily homeless.

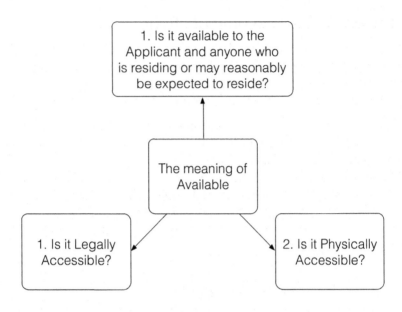

*Figure 10: The meaning of 'available'*

This and all criteria equally apply if any of the above are likely (not necessarily definitely will, note) to become true within the next 28 days.

Accommodation must be physically accessible. This is similar in practice to the test of 'can entry be secured'. It does not matter what the applicant 'could do'; the test is: is the accommodation available at the time of application or approach to the local authority. Can entry be secured now? The local authority might assist the person to gain entry but if they do not, they cannot refuse a duty purely on the grounds that the applicant has failed to take action themselves; there could be any number of reasons why this might be not be able to do so.

Grounds for challenge can rest on being unable to afford to travel back to accommodation if located in another country, but local authorities will often pay the air fare if this works out cheaper than providing temporary accommodation or paying for the rent and deposit on a private tenancy.

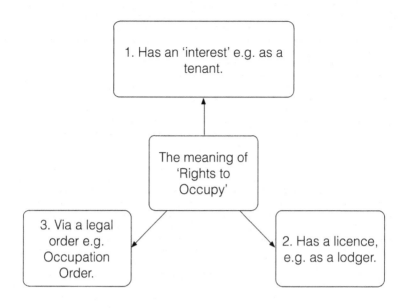

1. Has an 'interest' e.g. as a tenant.

The meaning of 'Rights to Occupy'

3. Via a legal order e.g. Occupation Order.

2. Has a licence, e.g. as a lodger.

*Figure 11: The meaning of 'rights to occupy'*

# 4. To which there are some rights to occupy?

It is usually clear if a person has some rights to occupy a property but the boundary can become blurred when it comes to tenancy rights. When does a person actually become homeless from a tenancy? According to case law, it is not until all rights of occupation have been exhausted; i.e. when a bailiffs warrant is being executed. Neither a s21 Notice To Quit nor a Possession Order render a person homeless by themselves.

If a local authority insists on taking this approach with your client there are two defences:

1. You can argue that it is not reasonable for your client to remain until the execution of a bailiffs warrant. This could be for reasons of risk of harassment from a landlord, the client being liable for the landlord's court fees or perhaps stress exacerbating a health condition. In this instance, it is highly subjective as to what is 'reasonable'.

2. Better, is to challenge the local authority on an Administrative Principle of law. In this case look to see if this is what the local authority always do. If so, they may be guilty of carrying out what is called 'a blanket policy'. If they have not shown why they consider it is reasonable for your client to remain until the bailiffs arrive, having considered the individual circumstances of this case, then their actions may be challengeable.

A common right to occupy is simply by way of permission, from the owners, relatives, friends who were allowing the person to stay there initially. This can be withdrawn at anytime and can be done so verbally; it does not have to be in writing. A local authority will often contact those with whom an applicant has been staying. If they confirm over the phone that they will no longer allow either the applicant or someone with whom the applicant can be reasonably expected to reside with, to stay then there is nothing the authority can do about it and, all else being equal, they must consider that person homeless.

## 5. To which entry can be secured?
This does not come into play very often except in one circumstance; where someone is excluded by another resident; typically a spouse or partner.

If this situation applies or can be held to apply, then it will usually be argued that, while legal remedies could be applied to enforce entry against the other party's wishes, to do so would render the applicant at risk of violence or threats of likely to be carried out. The accommodation therefore is unreasonable to occupy and the person is therefore homeless on that basis. This is how to argue this scenario.

## 6. If it is a movable structure, is there somewhere it can be parked or moored?
This is an unusual scenario and I have never seen it used in practice as a basis on which to prove homelessness. Which is strange, given its applicability to those living in vehicles, caravans or on boats.

Case law has decided that a waterways licence was 'permission to cruise the waterways'; an equivalent to a vehicle's roads tax. On that basis, it would appear that in theory, anyone with a legally taxed or licenced vehicle or boat, who has nowhere that they can legally park or moor it, is technically homeless.

If using this as a basis for demonstrating homelessness, the first thing the homeless officer is going to do is to look at the previous accommodation and look for a basis for intentionality - why did the person leave their last accommodation and become homeless? You must therefore also delve into the person's accommodation history and iron this out. Any grounds for a potential finding of intentionality must counter challenges - see the section on intentionality for this. Typically they will revolve around arguments that the earlier accommodation was not reasonable to occupy. But remember to keep going back until you arrive at the *last settled accommodation* - the homeless officer will. It is this that accommodation that you must demonstrate was not left intentionally.

# 7. Is it reasonable to occupy?

Even if all the other tests apply, if accommodation is not reasonable to occupy then a person is homeless. This is usually the main focus of any challenge and as shown in figure 12, there are three main aspects to this challenge.

## i. Risk Of Violence

Violence is defined widely and domestic violence in particular includes threatening behaviour, psychological, physical, sexual, financial and emotional abuse. The test is whether a person is at risk; they are not required to actually suffer violence in order to come within this test. It also includes threats likely to be carried out and general harassment. Accommodation cannot be considered as reasonable to occupy if you or anyone you live with or might reasonably be expected to live with, might be at risk of violence or threats of violence likely to be carried out, whilst living there.

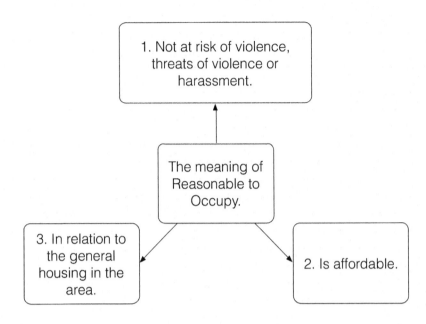

Figure 12: The meaning of 'reasonable to occupy'

This is a low standard of proof and you are not required to do anything to stop the violence or threats. So it does not matter if you have not gone to the police nor if you have not taken out any injunctions against any instigator of any threats. It does not matter if you have not reported any events to your landlord or the police or any other organisations, though doing so would undoubtedly be advisable. It is only necessary for there to be violence or threats of violence likely to be carried out for your accommodation to be considered unreasonable to occupy. The violence of threats of violence do not have to come from anyone living in the same property as you, and they can be directed against anyone living with you or anyone who might reasonably be expected to live with you.

This is a very common reason for people applying as and being accepted as, homeless. Because the standard of proof is so low it is very difficult for a local council to rule against someone claiming homelessness for this reason. Though not essential, it is always useful to gather police reports and confirmation of any incidents from other professionals such as health visitors, medical staff or social workers. If an applicant has reported an incident then it is in effect confirmation that it happened.

## ii.Affordability

Affordability is mandatory for the local authority to investigate and assess for every approach. If they have not done so or not shown that they have done so, then any refusal of duty is automatically flawed and is directly challengeable as a result.

Each local authority is likely to carry out an affordability assessment in their own way as there is no definitive standard of what is affordable as such. If the local authority consider a property to be affordable it is for you to show why it is not. The local authority has only to reach a decision which is 'reasonable'. However, it must take into account the following:

• The financial resources available to the applicant.

• The costs in respect of the accommodation.

• The existence of any maintenance payments.

• Reasonable living expenses.

If they have not done this then any affordability assessment has not been done correctly according to the legislation and is flawed and therefore would not be able to be defended if challenged.

## iii. General Housing Conditions

Only challengeable if an applicant's housing condition can be considered to be unreasonably worse than that typical in your local area. Statutory overcrowding does not in itself render accommodation unreasonable to occupy, though it may be used as a contributing factor. Request an assessment from the local authority's private sector or environmental health team first - the local authority often will and their assessment carries professional weight.

Look at the impact on a person's health and gather reports from health professionals.  However - if this is a strong factor, it may be far more useful to focus on requesting that the local authority issue a housing order on the property due to the duties to rehouse and potentially compensate your client as a result.

## Housing Orders

It is always beneficial to investigate if there are grounds for a housing order being issued due to the benefits they can confer on a resident subject to them. If a housing order is issued which displaces your client from their accommodation, under the Land Compensation Act s39 the local authority have a duty to provide the applicant with suitable, alternative accommodation. This can be either in the private sector or from the 'waiting list' of social housing, effectively as a direct nomination: i.e. they go to the top of the list, in effect. If the applicant has lived in the property for at least one year, then the local authority is also obliged to pay each displaced resident £4000 in compensation.

This is not part of the homelessness legislation but is a little known duty which can often be relevant to those in poor standard accommodation who may not come within the statutory homelessness safety net. It is hardly ever used and even local authority staff may not be aware of it. As such, it is always worth investigating alongside any homelessness enquiry. You may need to remind your local authority of their duties to an applicant in this regard.

Housing orders cover a variety of notices which a local authority can issue due to a Category 1 or 2 hazard being found. The calculation of this is complex and the full guidance can be found here:

*https://www.gov.uk/government/uploads/system/uploads/attachment_data/file/15810/142631.pdf*

Bitly link: *http://bit.ly/1gp8MOB*

# 9. Priority Need

Even if a person is homeless, a local authority only have a duty to provide accommodation if that person has what is called a 'priority need'. Though set out in legislation in a rather complicated fashion, really there are just two types of priority need: those in which the priority need is automatic and those in which it is discretionary.

If a person meets the criteria for the automatic category, then the council has no choice in classifying them as having a priority need. This is usually predominantly a matter of fact; one either 'is or isn't'. To gain a priority need under the discretionary tests, a person needs to be 'vulnerable' as a result of a specified causative factor.

## Key Concept: Ensure that the main applicant is the *One Without the Priority Need*

This might seem an odd piece of advice but it can have very beneficial consequences for applicants should their circumstances change after they have gained a full housing duty from a local authority. It stems from the following three elements of homelessness legislation.

One: where a person has a priority need, all other individuals who 'reside or might reasonably be expected to reside' with that person also have a priority need.

Two: once a local authority has made a decision accepting that a person has a priority need, they cannot reverse that decision, even if the applicant's circumstances change and they cease to have a priority need (apart from in cases of fraud). A common example here is a pregnant woman who ceases to be pregnant after a duty has been accepted to her; the duty continues.

Three: in homelessness, there is only one applicant.

Putting these elements together, if the main applicant for a household is the one without any priority need, then the local authority accepts a duty to them on the basis that they do have a priority need because someone they reside with or might reasonably be expected to reside with, has a priority need (e.g. a pregnant partner).

Once that decision is made, the local authority cannot reverse that decision or renege on that duty just because the applicant's circumstances have changed to make them cease to have a priority need. It makes no difference whether that change is a pregnant woman losing a pregnancy or a couple with a child separating or a member of a household recovering from an illness which initially gave them a priority need.

This principle works with any household who have a member with a priority need in their own right.

So, if advising a client, assess whether this is an option and if so, discuss with the client the advantages of ensuring that the person WITHOUT the priority need is the main applicant. You are, in effect, getting two or several housing duties (depending on the number of adults in the household) for one application.

What follows is a guide to each of the priority need tests and ways to challenge each one.

# Automatic Priority Need & How To Challenge

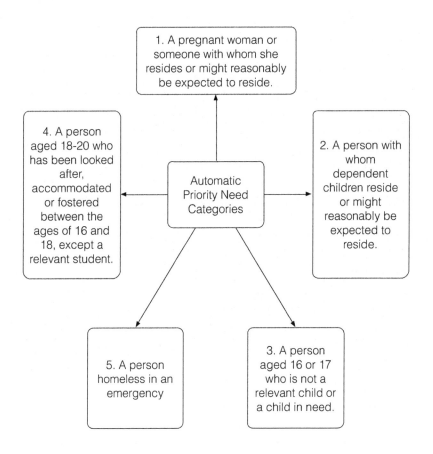

*Figure 13: The criteria for having an automatic priority need.*

## 1. Pregnancy

This is normally understood as simply meaning that a pregnant woman has an automatic priority need. Whilst true, the full test is "A pregnant woman or a person with whom she resides or might reasonably be expected to reside".

This is a very typical situation where the key concept of the 'non-priority main applicant' applies.

If an expectant couple apply as homeless and the actual applicant is the non-pregnant partner then if they subsequently split up, both partners will continue to enjoy a priority need and, barring exclusions on other grounds, the full housing duty.

Remembering that in homelessness there is only one applicant, if the main applicant is the non-pregnant partner then the local authority has already accepted that they have a priority need on the legal basis that someone they reside with or might reasonably be expected to reside with, has a priority need (i.e. their pregnant partner). Once that decision is made and the full housing duty accepted, the local authority cannot reverse that decision or renege on that duty just because the applicant's circumstances have changed to make them cease to have a priority need; i.e. their pregnant partner leaving them.

The pregnant partner here has an automatic priority need, so their rights are straightforward; should there be a change of circumstances in the future, they will be able to make a fresh application and, all else being equal,  will be automatically awarded the full housing duty, due to their automatic priority need.


## 2. Resident, Dependent Children

The test has two parts; whether children are actually residing and whether they might reasonably be expected to do so. Whilst fairly straightforward when children are living with their parent or parents, it becomes difficult in the case of split families.

Whilst children can reside with and be dependent on more than one person, the presumption is strongly against this. Local Authorities are not bound by court decisions on shared residency orders. They are entitled to make their own decision on this test.

A person will need to be able to demonstrate a range of evidence to show that they have resident, dependent children alongside another person. The following actions are recommended to build a body of evidence to support a client's claim:

Notify housing benefits that their children stay with them. This creates an official record which you can present to the housing department.

Ensure the children's school has your client's contact details in case of an emergency as well as the other parent and are instructed to call both parents. Evidence this in writing.

Do the same with the health clinic where the children are registered. Investigate any clubs or activities your client takes the child to. Evidence in writing that they have your client's contact details registered as the parent or main contact.

If your submissions can reference all of the above, it makes it much more difficult for a local authority to reach a decision that a person does not have priority need on the grounds that any children can not reasonably be expected to reside with a person.

Remember that a person can be classified as a dependent child up to the age of 19 if they are in full time education.

## 3. Aged 16 and 17

Though this age group have an automatic priority need under homelessness legislation, if representing such a client, a better course of action is to ignore the homeless route and instead focus one's efforts on the duties Social Services have under s20 of the 1989 Children Act.

The case of R (G) v London Borough of Southwark (2009), made it very clear that only in the most exceptional of cases would a homeless 16/17 year old not be dealt with by Social Services as a child in need (and the exceptions are truly exceptional).You have the full details of the Southwark case in your cloud folder and I recommend reading it in full.

Below is an overview of the main points to be aware of.

The definition of a 'Child In Need' under s17 is:
"A child shall be taken to be in need if:
    a) he is unlikely to achieve or maintain or to have the opportunity of achieving or maintaining, a reasonable standard of health or development without the provision for him of services by a local authority.
    b) his health or development is likely to be significantly impaired, or further impaired, without the provision for him of such services; or
    c) he is disabled."

Section 20 then goes on to say regarding the provision of accommodation:
"Every local authority shall provide accommodation for any child in need within their area who appears to them to require accommodation as a result of
    (a)there being no person who has parental responsibility for him;
    (b)his being lost or having been abandoned; or
    (c)the person who has been caring for him being prevented (whether or not permanently, and for whatever reason) from providing him with suitable accommodation or care."

If that wasn't clear enough, the Southwark case stated the following:
"Is the applicant a child in need? (Given the child is homeless, how could the answer be anything other than yes?)"
"In blunt terms, a local children's services authority cannot refer a homeless child in need to the local housing authority", and
"The House of Lords has reiterated that the Children's Act has primacy over the Housing Act in providing for children in need".

In view of the above, when dealing with a homeless 16 or 17 year old, there is only one goal; for the young person to be accepted as a 'Child in Need' and accommodated under s20 of the Children Act.

A response which you may encounter is the young person being offered a s17 duty only and referred back to the homeless department for accommodation. The young person will not then receive the same level of support nor for as long, as a person accommodated under s20. Unless you feel that this is the most appropriate option, do not accept accommodation under homelessness legislation; push for a full s20 duty.

It is very important to accompany the young person to their interview with Social Services and to be with them during the interview to help them to understand the advantages of a s20 Duty and the consequences of refusing it.

## 4. A person who has been looked after, accommodated or fostered and is aged under 21

Not normally contentious. This is predominantly a matter of checking the dates. One either does or does not come within this category. The following are the categories of 'care':

Looked after by a local authority as part of a care order or a voluntary agreement.

- Accommodated by a voluntary organisation.
- Accommodated in a private children's home.
- Accommodated for at least 3 consecutive months by
- - a health authority, special health authority, primary care trust or local education authority, or
- - in any care home or independent hospital or in any accommodation provided by a National Health Service trust.
- Privately fostered.

## 5. Homeless due to an emergency

This is not normally contentious. An emergency means a sudden event which renders a person's accommodation unsuitable to reside in. Flood, fire or other natural disasters come within this. They key is physical damage to such an extent that the accommodation is no longer viable.

Note that a local authority is not really entitled to push the responsibility for such a homeless person back to a landlord on the basis of 'a landlord's insurance' or any similar excuse. The legislation regarding landlord and tenant duties and obligations to each other in the event of a property being rendered suddenly uninhabitable is extremely complex and unclear, but the duty of a local authority towards such a person is very simple and very clear; it is an automatic priority need with a corresponding duty to accommodate.

# Discretionary Priority Need & How To Challenge

The so-called 'discretionary priority need categories' all share one characteristic in common: the concept of 'vulnerability'.

If a person does not fall into one of the automatic priority need categories then a local authority will only have a duty to provide accommodation for them if the person can show that they are 'vulnerable' as a result of one of the causes in these discretionary tests. Each of these tests has its own criteria of what a local authority should consider when assessing vulnerability, which you can use to structure your evidence and argument. We will look at each of these in turn.

## Vulnerability

This is the single most important concept in homelessness and it has a very specific meaning in the context of housing law.

The working definition has been the subject of much debate and subsequent case law. In 2015 the Supreme Court overturned the previous definition (known as the Pereira Test) and in the case of Hotak and others (Appellants) v London Borough of Southwark and another (Respondents) [2015] handed down a new working definition of vulnerability.

The court said that vulnerable means 'significantly more vulnerable than ordinarily vulnerable' and the correct comparison is with 'the ordinary person if rendered homeless'.

So vulnerability in the context of homeless law means showing that a person is: "significantly more vulnerable than an ordinary person (would be) if made homeless".

It is up to the local authority to decide whether or not a person meets this definition. It is a highly subjective and difficult decision; even the courts have recognised this. The evidence and arguments you submit will have a primary influence on the local authority's final decision.

The courts have also repeatedly stated that the decision on whether or not a person is vulnerable is one for the local authority alone to make. It is not one that the courts, medical staff or anyone else is qualified to or empowered by parliament to make. The key to success then is to submit such information

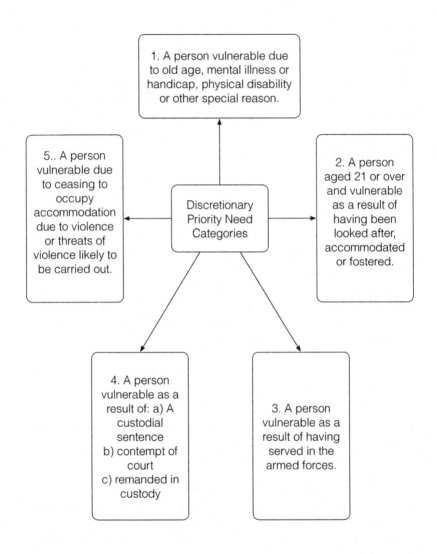

1. A person vulnerable due to old age, mental illness or handicap, physical disability or other special reason.

5.. A person vulnerable due to ceasing to occupy accommodation due to violence or threats of violence likely to be carried out.

Discretionary Priority Need Categories

2. A person aged 21 or over and vulnerable as a result of having been looked after, accommodated or fostered.

4. A person vulnerable as a result of: a) A custodial sentence b) contempt of court c) remanded in custody

3. A person vulnerable as a result of having served in the armed forces.

*Figure 14: The criteria for discretionary priority need.*

that the local authority cannot reach any other conclusion than that of accepting your client as vulnerable.

## Key Concept: Evidencing Vulnerability

When needing to show how a person is vulnerable, do not be distracted by any named medical diagnosis or condition. Instead, gather evidence around these two questions :

1. How does it affect them and

2. How do they cope with it.

Two individuals can have the same condition but one can be found vulnerable and the other not, depending on how they answer to the above two criteria. This is how you will evidence that a person is 'significantly more vulnerable'.

### General factors for showing vulnerability

In all vulnerability assessments, what a local authority is looking for, and what you should show, is evidence that a person copes less well when homeless than an 'ordinary' person would if homeless. Whatever the type of vulnerability, the following are factors you would usually be considering:

1. Evidence to show how a person or their condition is worse when homeless and improves when housed.

2. Evidence to show what support a person needs and how they will be unable to receive or access this if homeless.

3. Evidence to show a lack of skills and coping ability; i.e. which is less than an average homeless person.

### Look at the following:

1. Activities of daily living; i.e. the person's level of ability with washing, toileting, shopping, dealing with money, mobility issues.

2. Medical prognosis: whether or not a condition is degenerative, long term, debilitating now, what side affects any medication taken has, the level of any medication and whether or not this is higher or lower than average, whether

the dosage has increased over time.

You will find an example medical form and an Activities of Daily Living assessment form in your downloadable cloud pack.

## Gather Evidence

When representing a person, it is important to collect actual evidence for submission. Many organisations will attempt to challenge a local authority decision by submitting a body of information which is based only on the applicant's assertions. When the local authority investigates, it finds no or little evidence of these assertions and the person and the organisation representing them look less reliable as a result.

Because a local authority will always investigate, it is vitally important that you do as well. Seek written evidence from all relevant third parties of all of the factors mentioned above and all of the factors below in the specific tests for the discretionary priority need reasons.

Don't contact third party organisations, especially medical staff, to ask for their opinion; they are virtually guaranteed to say that their client is vulnerable. However, this is worthless for two reasons. Firstly, parliament has stated specifically that no one but the local authority is qualified or empowered to make a decision on whether or not a person is vulnerable. Not doctors, not psychiatrists, not anyone else. So when a professional says that they think a person is vulnerable it carries little weight in this content. Secondly, vulnerable has a specific meaning in homelessness and that is very unlikely to be the test a person's GP is applying. The local authority knows this and so do the courts.

Instead of asking a third party for their opinion, ask them for actual evidence relating to the specific tests of vulnerability. This is what a local authority will do and if you are to represent your client successfully, it is what you need to do as well.

## Don't do this:

It is common, when assessing homelessness applications, to receive letters of support from organisations representing an applicant which describes how well a person has done when homeless. They may detail how a person has reduced their drug or alcohol misuse, how they have engaged with services, perhaps taken up voluntary training or engaged with various support pathways. All this, even whilst homeless.

Such a letter effectively makes the 'non-priority need' decision for the local authority. You have just told them all they need to know about *how well this person is coping with being homeless* and therefore excluded them from the very definition of vulnerability. It is most unlikely that any person would receive a full housing duty after submitting a support letter of this nature.

## The Discretionary Priority Need Tests

Each discretionary priority need test has its own specific guidance for what a local authority should look at when assessing whether or not a person is vulnerable due to that specific reason.

Remember that for all of the following, they also apply to anyone who resides or may reasonably be expected to reside, with the applicant. So always look beyond your immediate client, to their wider social context.

The way each of the following tests work is by asking whether or not a person is *vulnerable due to*...x,y,z reason. The meaning of vulnerability is the same in each test; is the person significantly more vulnerable than an ordinary person if homeless.

The difference is that for each of the following tests, you can also show how a person is vulnerable as *a result of*, the 'causative factor' in each case; e.g. how being in the forces or being in care has made the person more vulnerable. These tests then provide extra reasons, with a related structure for your evidence, for showing how your client has a priority need.

These criteria form an incredibly useful framework for structuring what questions you ask your client, what questions you ask and evidence you request from any third party organisations or professionals involved with your client and for assessing any negative decision letter which the local authority might issue. Remember that if the local authority does not show that it has taken these criteria into consideration in making its decision, then that decision is flawed and challengeable on a number of administrative law grounds, such as:

1. The authority has taken into account irrelevant considerations, or omitted to take account of relevant considerations.

2. The authority has wrongly interpreted the law/misdirected itself.

3. The authority had operated a 'blanket' policy.

4. The authority should give a reasoned decision.

Now lets look at the different categories of discretionary priority need.


## 1. Vulnerable due to old age, mental illness or handicap, physical disability or other special reason

This is the main category for most claims of priority need. It existed before all of the more specific discretionary categories which were brought in by the 2002 Homelessness Act. If a person does not fall under any of those categories then this is the one to use because it covers most if not all other eventualities. To show how your client comes within this test, use the guides below to show how your client is vulnerable according to the definition below.

### Demonstrating a person is vulnerable due to old age

Old age does not confer an automatic priority need in itself. Use the general factors discussed above to show how your client is vulnerable due to age related matters. 60 years old is generally the threshold for age becoming relevant.

**Demonstrating a person is vulnerable due to mental illness, physical disability or any other special reason**

In considering whether or not a person is vulnerable (in housing terms), the local authority must look at the following factors. Make sure you structure your evidence to take account of these or to focus your challenge through these if the local authority has not made explicit reference to them in its original decision.

1. The nature and extent of the illness and/or disability which may render the applicant vulnerable.

2. The relationship between the illness and/or disability and the individual's housing difficulties.

3. The relationship between the illness and/or disability and other factors such as drug/alcohol misuse, offending behaviour, challenging behaviours, age and personality disorder.

The above factors give a structure to the relationship between the person's illness or disability and other factors. The third criteria makes it clear that any illness or disability may be exacerbated by compounding factors to make a person more vulnerable than they would be if they had only the illness or disability alone to contend with.


**2. Vulnerable due to having been looked after, accommodated or fostered and aged 21 or over.**

Look at the following factors when considering vulnerability for those who have been in care.

1. The length of time the person spent in care.

2. The reasons why the person was originally placed into care.

3. The length of time since leaving care & whether the person has been able to find & maintain accommodation in that time.

4. Whether the person has any positive support networks of friends or family.

## 3. Vulnerable due to having been a member of the armed forces

Look at the following factors when considering vulnerability for ex forces clients.

1. The length of time the person spent in the armed forces.

2. Whether the person was engaged in active service.

3. Whether the person spent any time in a military hospital, has post traumatic stress or other serious health problem related to military service.

4. Whether the person was judged to be vulnerable by HM Forces medical & welfare advisers and issued a Medical History Release form (F Med 133).

5. The length of time since the person left the armed forces and whether or not they have been able to find and maintain accommodation since that time.

6. The existence of any support networks of family or friends.

## 4. Vulnerable due to having been served a custodial sentence, been committed for contempt of court or remanded in custody

Use the following criteria when considering vulnerability for such clients.

1. The length of time served in custody.

2. Whether the person is receiving supervision from a criminal justice agency.

3. The length of time since the person was released from custody and the extent to which the person has been able to obtain and/or maintain accommodation during that time.

4. Whether the person has any positive support networks of friends or family.

## 5. Vulnerable due to having left accommodation due to violence or threats of violence likely to be carried out

Contrary to popular belief, being homeless due to violence,

domestic or otherwise, does not confer any automatic priority need. It is only if a person is vulnerable as a result of this, that a person might be awarded priority need status.

This normally only affects single people or childless couples. If a person is subject to violence then they are automatically homeless due to it not being reasonable to occupy accommodation in which one is at risk of violence or threats likely to be carried out. If such a person has children (or other automatic priority need) then this discretionary priority need test is never carried out; it is the children which passport the person through the priority need test.

If a person is homeless due to violence and they do not fall within any of the automatic priority need tests then they are faced with demonstrating that they are vulnerable as a result of the violence or threats of violence. Use the following criteria when assisting such clients.

1. The nature of the violence or threats of violence; whether a single but significant incident or a number of incidents over an extended time having a cumulative affect.

2. The impact and likely effects of the violence or threats of violence on the person's current and future well being.

3. Whether the person has any existing support networks or family or friends.

## How to Use These Challenges

Use the structures in each of these tests to guide your questioning of your client and any subsequent enquiries you make or questions you ask of third parties for more information.

If submitting this pre s184 level, you should not need to structure your information in this way to the local authority; after all, they should already know all of these tests. However, if you do not see these tests being explicitly dealt with in the s184 decision letter, then they should definitely be used as grounds for challenging that decision and to structure your review decisions.

There are arguments for not submitting such detailed information at all pre s184 decision. If you do, you run the risk that you are, in effect, doing the local authority's work for them and it is much easier for a local authority to reach a negative decision at s184 level than it is a s202 review level, if that is when you submit your really detailed and structured evidence.

A s202 review is typically carried out by a more experienced officer who will understand the ramifications and importance of submissions referencing the criteria in this section. They will have to present very robust arguments as to why your client does not meet the criteria, which may not be possible. Furthermore, if they do still reach a negative decision and you then threaten to go for as204 appeal and your review submissions have created a good strong case, then the local authorities chances of winning at court level will be much diminished. The review officer will know this and they will be advised of this by any barristers they consult. Not to mention the cost of a s204 appeal which they will want to avoid. The cheaper and easier option is to overturn the s184 decision at review level and accept your client.

When challenging at review level, tie your submissions in with the administrative principles which you are stating that the local authority has contravened.

# 10. Intentionality

## The 6 Point Test of Intentionality

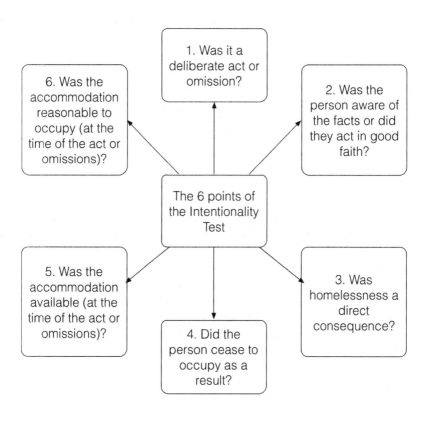

*Figure 15: The 6 point intentionality test.*

Just as the concept of 'priority need' is based on the notion of the 'needy poor', so the concept of 'intentionality' is based on the concept of the 'deserving poor'; the corollary being that help is only available to those whose homelessness is not 'their own fault'. It is a misleadingly named test; of course, no one deliberately sets out to 'make themselves homeless. Rather, it seeks to distinguish those who are homeless as a result of their own actions or inactions. This could, in theory, include virtually everyone, so it is mediated by the 6 points above, each one of which must be in the affirmative, to bring a person within its remit.

Despite its somewhat fearsome reputation, intentionality is a relatively easy test to circumnavigate. If you can answer 'no' to just one of the 6 points then you cannot be considered to be homeless intentionally. This is also a test which local authorities get wrong very frequently and officers find very confusing because they do not use this 6-point structure to make their decisions. Make sure you use it to structure your challenge letter to overturn a s184 decision.

## Challenging Intentionality

### 1. Deliberate Act or Omission
### a) Where the act was a temporary aberration
If the act or omission was the result of a temporary aberration in behaviour, or a result of a limited mental capacity or caused by a mental illness or caused by an assessed substance abuse, then it cannot be considered to be a deliberate act which renders the person intentionally homeless.

There is much in here for successful challenges to homelessness decisions but in reality it has been very little used. A very common use would be where depression caused a lack of action. Anyone assessed as having a substance misuse behaviour would be exempt from being found to be intentional, if the act or omission was as a result of this substance misuse. Even a temporary aberration in behaviour, with no apparent cause, is enough to lift one out of being caught by this test.

Always question your client on these issues, gain testimony from medical professionals, friends, family, neighbours, other professionals & employers. Look at issues of stress, mental illness in its widest sense and any side affects of medication, to show how your client is within these exclusions.

## b) Financial difficulties outside your client's control

This also is an exclusion. Eviction for non payment of rent due to delays in Housing Benefit (HB), payments do not render a person intentionally homeless. It is important here that there is no evidence that a person has not responded to any requests for information from the HB department; a person would not be excluded in that case. Always ask for any receipts to confirm that any information has been submitted to the local authority.

Non payment of mortgage due to business or credit delays, withholding of rent or mortgage payments by a partner, which the applicant could not influence, could all be considered under this exclusion.

## c) Duress

Acts or omissions made under duress are specifically excluded from being considered. Consider any pressure from creditors where individuals experience pressure to make payments to creditors rather than paying their rent. Pressure from abusive partners or behaviour influenced by peers or third parties which exert control over your client. All of these would exclude your client from being found to be homeless intentionally.

Where an applicant is incapable of managing their own affairs, they are also excluded from the intentionality test. However, this should normally be fairly obvious. However, this clause could be used to exclude a person on the grounds of old age, disability or the side affects of medication.

## 2. Awareness of the facts or acted in good faith

There are no specific challenges to this clause; it is very much on a case by case basis and dependent on showing how your client was unaware of a relevant material fact.

Ignorance of ability to claim benefits is often attempted but if an applicant has previously claimed benefits then it is reasonable for the local authority to assume awareness.

Leaving a tenancy or selling a property where there exist possession proceedings to which there is no defence, is to be considered a 'good faith' act and will not render a person intentionally homeless by itself.

### 3. Was homelessness a direct consequence?
The courts have observed that "causation (is) a notorious minefield in jurisprudence and philosophy". The local authority must be able to show a direct causal link between the deliberate act and the homelessness. If it cannot, then a person is not intentionally homeless.

Strike up a conversation with the landlord or evicting agent. Exactly why did they issue notice? Was it for some reason other than the proposed 'act or omission'? If the evicting agent states another reason, then it is not possible for the local authority to reach an intentionality decision.

Examine the chain of events from the proposed deliberate act and the event of becoming homeless. Was homelessness an inevitable consequence? If not, it can be argued both that homelessness was not a direct consequence and that the applicant acted in good faith, because it could not be known that homelessness would be a result.

### 4. Did the applicant cease to occupy?
This is confusingly closely related to the previous test and is normally somewhat glossed over. Did the person cease to occupy as a result of the deliberate act or omission?

One common scenario is where a parent sells their house to their adult child and then rents it off them. Subsequently, the son or daughter issues a notice to quit. This is not intentional (unless deliberate collusion can be proven) because the act which caused the homelessness was not the sale of the property but the issuing of a notice.

As a corollary to this, a person can rarely be found to be homeless intentionally from accommodation they were not occupying. Sometimes a local authority will try to reach a finding of intentionality where a person fails to take up accommodation made available to them. The one exception to this is if the person had gone as far as signing up for the property and accepting the keys. In this situation, it has been held that even though the person was not actually occupying the property, they had 'notional' occupation of it and their subsequent homelessness was as a failure to make use of that 'occupational right'.

### 5. Was the accommodation available?

This has the same meaning here as in the earlier test for homelessness. Therefore, if a person has been excluded by a partner and then stops paying rent because they are not living their, neither partner would be considered to be homeless intentionally. Where this applies it can be very useful for excluding people from being caught by this test.

### 6. Was the accommodation reasonable to occupy?

This has the same meaning here as in the earlier test for homelessness. Accommodation cannot be considered as reasonable to occupy if:

1. The person or anyone with whom they reside or might reasonably be expected to reside, is at risk of violence or threats of violence likely to be carried out, at that property.

2. The accommodation is not affordable.

3. The accommodation is not reasonable to occupy on account of its condition.

Lets have a look at these in turn, because they are all excellent means of challenging and overturning a decision that someone is homeless intentionally.

1. If a person is at risk of violence or threats of violence likely to be carried out, then the accommodation is not reasonable to occupy and therefore they cannot be found to be intentionally homeless from such accommodation.

This test has, for obvious reasons, a low threshold of proof, as it not always possible to provide proof of being at risk of violence. However, if a person has reported incidents or concerns to any third parties such as schools, social services, medical staff, neighbours, friends or the police, then such a claim is likely to be accepted.

It is not necessary that the applicant has done anything to try to alleviate any violence or threats of such, nor can any applicant be required to do so.

2. If the accommodation is not affordable, then that accommodation is not reasonable to occupy and therefore they cannot be found to be intentionally homeless from such accommodation.

Remember that affordability is mandatory for a LA to make enquiries into and show that it has made enquiries into. If it has not considered this aspect in direct relation to your client's finances, then any decision on intentionality is flawed and instantly challengeable.

This will often be a single short sentence in a decision letter. Challenge this. The local authority has an obligation to investigate and assess your particular client's finances individually and to assess whether that property was affordable by that person. Whilst it is the local authority's decision as to whether or not a property is affordable, you can influence the local authority's decision if you can provide detailed financial information demonstrating why that property was not affordable by that person.

3. If the accommodation is of a condition such that it is not reasonable to occupy then a person cannot be found to be intentionally homeless from such accommodation.

As in homelessness, this is in relation to the general condition of housing in the district. Overcrowding can here carry greater weight. Whilst it may not be enough to render a person statutorily homeless, it can be enough to render accommodation unreasonable to occupy, such that they could not be found to be intentionally homeless for losing it.

Be wary with this exclusion however. If a person's last accommodation is found to be unreasonable to occupy, then it is open to the local authority to treat it as 'unsettled' and to look further back, to their last settled accommodation and find a person intentionally homeless from this, earlier accommodation. However, this is a double-edged sword; you too can argue that current accommodation is not reasonable to occupy and that therefore your client is in fact homeless from earlier accommodation, which they clearly lost through no fault of their own.

This can lead to the strange but not uncommon situation where a local authority is arguing that a person's last accommodation was reasonable to occupy, so that they can find them intentionally homeless, and you are arguing that it is not, so that the person is excluded. If you can make use of this, it is often one of the easiest ways around intentionality.

## General Ways Around Intentionality
As well as challenges to the 6 tests themselves, there are some more general ways to sidestep the entire intentionality test itself or to at least somewhat alleviate its affects.

### 1. Can another person apply as the main applicant?
This can be a dependent child, aged 16 or above, a partner, a relative or anyone who resides or might reasonably be expected to reside. It is the easiest way around intentionality.

Remember that in homelessness legislation there is only one applicant. The finding of intentionality is focussed on the person who is that main applicant. If another person applies, to whom the criteria do not apply, then the local authority will be frustrated in any attempt to apply a finding of intentionality to that application.

The main thing to watch for if doing this is with partners. It is open to a local authority to presume that a partner acquiesced in their partner's 'deliberate act or omission' for example. Unless you have clear evidence that one partner was not aware of what their partner was doing or that they protested against it, it is far better to use another family member if at all possible.

## 2. Use the residence clause to show how accommodation was not reasonable to occupy.

Remember that accommodation must be reasonable to occupy not just for the applicant but for anyone residing with them or for anyone who might reasonably be expected to reside with them.

It does not matter what the deliberate act or omission was, if the accommodation was not reasonable to occupy for a partner or another relative or family member, on grounds of size, health reasons, risk of violence or any other reason, then a finding of intentionality cannot be made.

## 3. Challenge the amount of time given in temporary accommodation.

When a local authority makes a finding of intentionally homeless, it is obliged to provide accommodation for a time reasonable to allow that person to find alternative accommodation. Typically, a local authority will provide accommodation for 7 days for a single person and 28 days for a family. This is highly open to challenge and has been done so in the courts on a number of occasions.

The 28 days has been extended up to 6 months, which illustrates the flexibility the local authority should take with this duty. If your local authority typically applies 28 days then they are breaking two Administrative Principles; not acting reasonably and applying a blanket policy.

Challenging this is by way of Judicial Review and an initial letter should be sufficient. There is little defence and it is not worth the local authority trying to defend, particularly if it does always offer 28 days after an intentionality decision and you can evidence this with previous decision letters.

Ask for three things;

   1: an extension of time in temporary accommodation sufficient to be reasonable for your client to find accommodation,

   2: practical assistance from the local authority to help your client find accommodation, through their contacts with landlords, and

3: financial assistance in paying for any accommodation found in the form of 'homeless relief'. This is a type of prevention which Local Authorities are able to provide following a negative decision. It is not obligatory but they are encouraged to do so by central government. A complaint to the Department of Communities and Local Government as to why your local authority is refusing to provide such assistance would result in very unwelcome attention from central government on your local authority. They will wish to avoid it.

# 11. Local Connection

The last of the 5 tests and the only one which a local authority is not legally required to look at if it does not wish to. Of course, in reality, every local authority will look at this aspect of a person's application. Local connection is mostly a matter of fact; one either has it or one doesn't, so it's not usually an area that contains many aspects to challenge.

The quickest way to gain a local connection is to find work in an area. Whilst not automatic, most local authority staff don't know this and will treat it as if it is.

Two concepts we have already looked at can be applied to local connection.

Firstly, a local connection can be gained not just by the applicant but on the basis of anyone who lives with the applicant or might reasonably be expected to reside with the applicant.

Normally, this is taken to mean close and immediate relatives and anyone else is pretty much automatically discarded. Don't let them be. Any relative can grant a local connection - but it is up to you to show the strength of the relationship between your applicant and this other relative, the connection between them and the importance of them being able to live in the same area.

Secondly, if a person is at risk to violence or threats of violence likely to be carried out, then they can apply to any other local authority and will not be at risk of a referral back to their original authority due to the risk of violence.

For both of these challenges, all the previously discussed criteria apply.

There is one aspect to examining a person's local connection which is little used and up to the local authority's discretion: the requirement to assess where there is 'any other special reason' why a person needs to be in a certain area.

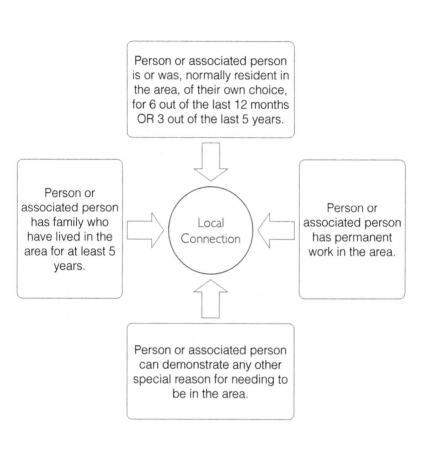

*Figure 16: The Local Connection criteria.*

The usual example of this is medical treatment only available in that local authority's area, or at least, not anywhere else close. But this can be anything and the local authority has to take it into account and assess it.

For all of these, if the local authority reject your reasons for local connection in their decision letter; don't worry. You will request a review and show how inadequate the local authority's initial decision was. The better your challenge letter the less chance the local authority is going to want to take it further if that's what you threaten. But we're getting ahead of ourselves; we will look at this later on.

So that's the 5 main tests. Next we're going to look at a little used power to accommodate, which is something which every person needing accommodation and every person advising such a person, needs to know about.

# 12. Powers To Accommodate

## 1. Following a Non Priority and Non Intentionally Homeless Decision

Sometimes, local authorities have powers to accommodate, as well as duties to accommodate. One of these was introduced by the 2002 Homelessness Act and has been little used and little challenged. The interesting aspect of powers is that, based on the Administrative Principles, if a local authority has a power, then they have a duty to consider using it, and show that they have considered using it, even if they decide not to use it in a particular case. They must then also show why they have not considered using it.

The power introduced in 2002 was the power under s192(3) of the 1996 Housing Act (as amended by the 2002 Homeless Act), to provide accommodation to those whom a local authority had found to be not homeless intentionally and not in priority need.

The challenge here is focussed not on the fact that accommodation has not been provided but on the way that the local authority has behaved.

If your client has received a non-priority decision letter, check to see if the local authority have stated in it that they have also examined intentionality and do not consider your client to be intentionally homeless and that they have also considered their power to provide accommodation and have, in this case, decided to not exercise their discretion to provide such accommodation and why.

If the decision letter does not have such a clause, then the decision is unlawful and open to challenge, ultimately by way of judicial review.

Initially, contact your local authority and request that they exercise their power to accommodate your client. Point out that they have not abided by the principles of administrative law in not explicitly stating that they have considered using this power nor why they have decided to not exercise this power. As such, their decision is flawed. State that your require accommodation for a reasonable time and that if it is not provided, you will be seeking application for judicial review.

This initial request should be all that is required. No local authority would win at a Judicial Review hearing on this and it is not worth challenging your request. You should not even have to go to the formal pre-action letter for this.

Of course, in reality, what is likely to happen is that fairly quickly your local authority will begin stating in its decision letters that it has looked at using this power but has decided not to do so in this case.

You will then be looking at challenging on the grounds that, if your local authority never exercises its power, it is in effect, exercising a blanket policy. Which is directly challengeable.

## 2. Pending the Outcome of a S202 Review

This is the second power which it is very important to know about.

As soon as the s202 review process is initiated, then the local authority have a power to provide accommodation to the person, pending the final review decision.

This is slightly different to the first power we looked at, in two ways. Firstly, it applies no matter what the original decision. Secondly, it has a definite structure which the local authority must consider when deciding whether or not to accommodate your client. It is this structure which you will use to either show the local authority that they should accommodate your client or to challenge their decision not to.

The test is known by a variety of names, based on the case laws which defined the criteria. You may hear them referred to as the 'Mohammed' or 'Camden' principles or the 'Nacion' principles.

### The Nacion test for accommodation pending a s202 review decision.

When considering whether or not to accommodate a person pending a review decision, the local authority must consider the following:

1. The merits of the case that the decision being challenged is flawed, including whether that decision appears contrary to the merits of the applicant's case and/or is finely balanced.

2. Any new information or arguments put forward which may have a real effect on the authority's decision.

3. The personal circumstances of the applicant and the consequences for them of an adverse decision on the exercise of this discretion.

4. Any other relevant considerations.

As with the discretionary priority need structures, you would not explicitly use these when first submitting your request for accommodation. The local authority should know enough to interpret your information against these criteria and issue a decision showing how they have done so. However, if they do not do this, and simply state that they will not be providing accommodation, then you would explicitly use these criteria and show how the local authority has failed to make proper consideration of the relevant issues in the right way and that therefore their decision is unlawful and directly challengeable by Judicial Review, which you will be seeking if they do not provide accommodation for your client forthwith.

If the local authority do use this structure when responding to requests for accommodation then a challenge is only likely to be possible if their refusal is clearly unreasonable. With public law, most of the challenges focus on the procedure, not the end decision. So if the local authority has gone about its duties in the right way, it is much more difficult to mount a successful challenge, even if the decision for your client is a negative one. However, the same comments about the use (or threatened use) of judicial review also apply here, so it is always worthy challenging any negative decision.

# 13. s202 Review Decisions

If you disagree with the initial s184 level decision on a homeless application, you can request that this decision is formally reviewed under s202. This is not yet at court level, though they do have a definite structure which it is worth learning in-order to better assist your client.

## What Decisions Can Be Reviewed
- Any decision on Eligibility.

- Any decision on Homelessness, Intentionality & Priority Need.

- Any decision on Local Connection. s198(5)

- A decision to Refer to another Authority. s198(1) & s200(4)

- Any decision on suitability of accommodation offered under Part 7.

- Any decision on the discharge of any duty.

## What Decisions Cannot Be Reviewed
- The suitability of accommodation offered under s188 pre-decision.

- The suitability of accommodation offered pending a local connection referral.

- Accommodation offered under a Power, pending a s202 review.

- Accommodation offered to non priority, unintentionally homeless.

- Accommodation offered pending a local connection referral review.

- Accommodation offered under Part 6 that is not an ending of a Part 7 duty (this is a suitability review instead, not a homelessness one).

# The Review Process & Time-line

When you or your client receive a decision letter (usually known as the s184 letter), it should contain a statement regarding your right to request a review of that decision and who to address your request to. Initiating the s202 review process is as easy as requesting one. There is no set format but it is usually better to submit a request in writing (including email) to avoid any confusion.

You have 21 days from the date a s184 decision letter is issued to request a review. While the local authority should be flexible regarding late requests, it is better to submit a request within the time limit. Make sure you are authorised by your client to also receive a copy of the decision as soon as it is issued.

Once you have requested a review, the local authority will give you a time-scale in which to submit any representations. This can be 14 days or 21 days; it varies with each authority. This time-scale is not statutory; in theory, extra information can be submitted right up until the actual decision is made and the local authority must take it into account. In practice however, you do not know exactly when a decision is going to be made and it helps both parties to agree a set date by which all submissions will be in. This date is however very flexible and it is very common for it to be extended due to various delays in obtaining required information. If you need more time; ask for it. It should not be refused.

Once a s202 review decision has been issued then the next formal challenge is by way of a s204 appeal to the County Court. This is not something to be undertaken lightly and for this you will absolutely require professional legal assistance to bring such a case.

However, if you really do believe that a s202 review decision is flawed, you can deal with it in the same manner as explained for Judicial Reviews above.

Submit a formal letter explaining why you consider the review to be flawed. State the points of law you are basing your case on (use the Administrative Principles for this). Invite the local authority to take a fresh application, especially if you have fresh

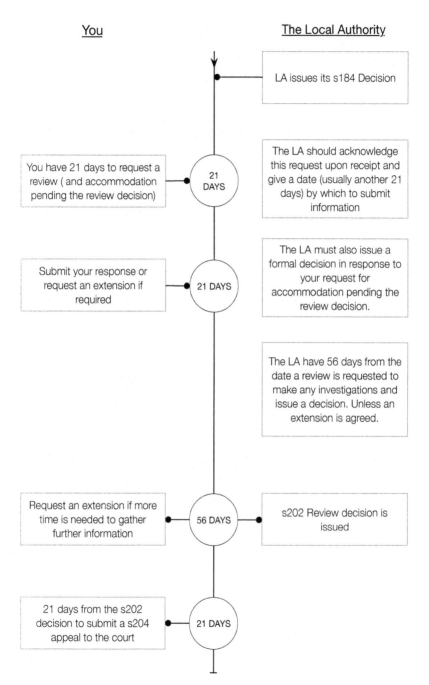

## You

## The Local Authority

LA issues its s184 Decision

You have 21 days to request a review ( and accommodation pending the review decision)

21 DAYS

The LA should acknowledge this request upon receipt and give a date (usually another 21 days) by which to submit information

Submit your response or request an extension if required

21 DAYS

The LA must also issue a formal decision in response to your request for accommodation pending the review decision.

The LA have 56 days from the date a review is requested to make any investigations and issue a decision. Unless an extension is agreed.

Request an extension if more time is needed to gather further information

56 DAYS

s202 Review decision is issued

21 days from the s202 decision to submit a s204 appeal to the court

21 DAYS

*Figure 17: The s202 Review Time-line.*

information to submit. State that if they do not, you will be seeking leave for a s204 appeal.

Few local authorities can afford to incur the cost of a s204 appeal, though some will on occasion. If you are able to offer an alternative, with polite but firm insistence and good grounds on paper, then it is in the local authority's interest to acquiesce and take a fresh application, most of the time. Not always though! This is how case law is made.

# How To Challenge & Win Reviews

As stated at the end of the chapter on vulnerability, there are arguments for waiting until a s202 review before using the structured tests we have looked at to inform your submissions.

One the simplest level, s184 decisions should not need such a formal approach and the presumption is that the correct decision will be reached at that initial level. The review is the final stage before court and should, in theory, only be necessary where something has gone wrong.

In reality, due to the sheer number of applications to some authorities, it is at the s202 review level where the real decision making happens. Hence the arguments for making more detailed and structured submissions only at this stage because they may be rather wasted if submitted at s184 level if decisions there are typically negative regardless of what is submitted.

## The s184 decision letter: the basis of your challenge

s184 of the 1996 Housing Act Part VII; the part that deals with homelessness, covers the duty on a local authority to investigate every claim for homelessness assistance made to it and to issue a decision letter at the end of that process.

The decision letter must set out what investigations were carried out, what evidence was obtained and, not just what the local authority's decision is but, crucially, how it has reached that decision; its reasoning, what it is based on. If it does not do this, then the decision is unlawful and can be challenged.

There is a great deal of case law just on decision letters alone. The following excepts should give you an idea of how s184 decision letters should be written (but all too often rarely are).

## Case Law on inadequate decision letters

R v Kensington and Chelsea RLBC ex p Kassam 1994

"All to often, in my experience, authorities do not give reasons which are sufficient within (s184), ...If they do not give sufficient reasons it is not surprising that they will face challenges. This only assists the lawyers and leads to further delays and expense.

To a large extent, the remedy lies in the hands of the local authority."

R v Camden LBC ex p Adair 1997
This non-priority need decision was overturned because the decision letter; "did no more than recite a general formula, was totally devoid of reasoning and did not state why the council did not consider (the person) to be vulnerable or what enquiries had been made".

R v Ealing LBC ex p Chanter 1992
This Intentionality decision was overturned because adverse information was not put to the applicant before the decision was made. "The failure to obtain the applicant's comments was a breach of natural justice and a failure to make appropriate enquiries".

R v Islington LBC ex p Trail 1993
In this case, the judge stated the reasons why a decision letter should give the reasons behind the decision.

1. it provides a valuable discipline for decision-takers,

2. it enables applicants to understand clearly why they have been unsuccessful and

3. it enables an assessment to be made of the prospects of challenge by further appeal or judicial review.

A simple recital of the routes to priority would be an obvious failure of comply with the duty.

Simpson v Brent LBC 2000
In this case, the non priority need decision letter set out its 'reasoning' over just 6 lines. Unsurprisingly, the applicant requested a review of this decision.

The review letter on the face of it corrected all of the mistakes in the initial decision letter; it set out the investigations that had been carried out, the reasoning which had been followed in the decision making and concluded with the serious decision that the applicant and his partner had colluded to defraud the council into obtaining social housing. Yet the decision was overturned at court and the council lost. Why?

Because all of this information had been known at the date of the original decision but had not been mentioned in it. "The appellant had thus not had the opportunity he should have had to deal with it on review."

# What each decision letter should contain

It is clear then that the challenge to any negative decision is initially focussed on the s184 decision letter. It should clearly show the following four aspects:

1. What enquiries have been made.

2. What evidence has been gathered.

3. What tests have been applied.

4. The reasoning behind the decision: how the final decision is based on all of the above.

If all of the above are not clear, then on the principle of natural justice, the decision is flawed, because a person needs to be able to see how an authority reached their decision. They need to see what evidence it was based on, in case the local authority missed something that was relevant or took into account something that was irrelevant. A person needs to be able to see what investigations a local authority carried out, in order to be satisfied that all relevant individuals or organisations who could provide useful information have been contacted. Finally, a person needs to know what tests have been applied and to be able to see the reasoning behind the local authority's decision; how they have reached their decision. The reasoning might be incorrect or flawed and therefore challengeable.

In all of this, because homelessness legislation is administrative law, the challenge is almost always on how a decision has been reached, rather than on the nature of the decision itself. It is all about procedure rather than the end result.

Your first task then is to examine the decision letter and check that it is explicit regarding all of the above. Refer to all of the structures and criteria we have looked at for each of the 5 tests of homelessness. They should all be there in the decision letter (for each one that is relevant). If they are not, you know where to focus your challenge.

## s8, Minded-to and Oral Hearings

If a review officer considers that an initial s184 decision is flawed in some way, but they are still 'minded to' make a decision which is against the applicant's interests, then under 'Regulation 8', they must contact the applicant, explain the decision that they are minded to make and why, and invite the applicant or their representative, to make either written or oral representations or both, within a reasonable time frame.

Deficiencies or irregularities include:

1. failure to take into account relevant considerations and to ignore irrelevant ones;

2. failure to base the decision on the facts;

3. bad faith or dishonesty;

4. mistake of law;

5. decisions that run contrary to the policy of the 1996 Act;

6. irrationality or unreasonableness;

7. procedural unfairness, e.g. where an applicant has not been given a chance to comment on matters relevant to a decision.

It is the local authority 's decision as to whether or not an original decision was flawed so that Regulation 8 is triggered. If the authority do not believe that it is, then you may have to request an oral hearing yourself. Oral hearings are not mandatory, but local authorities are strongly advised to offer them. Many will do so as a matter of standard procedure whether they consider Regulation 8 applies or not.

Oral hearings can vary widely in their tone, from informal and friendly to almost tribunal like in formality. It is best to not let a client attend alone. Prepare thoroughly in terms of knowing your client's circumstances, the legal tests being discussed and any relevant information you have. Focus on the areas of inconsistency or incompleteness in the local authority's procedures and use the structures of the 5 tests and the principles of administrative law to show either how the local authority has failed to carry out its duties according to correct procedure or, how your client is owed a full housing duty.

If a case has gone as far as a review then it is likely to be concerned with a subjective judgement of a person's situation, rather than proving an 'either or' decision. It is therefore very open to argument, relevant submissions and subjective views of interpretation. All within the structures outlined previously for each of the tests.

It is not just final decisions that you can challenge with the s202 review process. Any discharge of duty which the local authority carries out under the homelessness legislation is also open to challenge by this process. It is a very important part of assisting a person into housing,; by making sure they either do not lose their temporary accommodation or are not offered accommodation which is unsuitable for them. We will look at this next.

# 14. Challenging Discharges of Duty

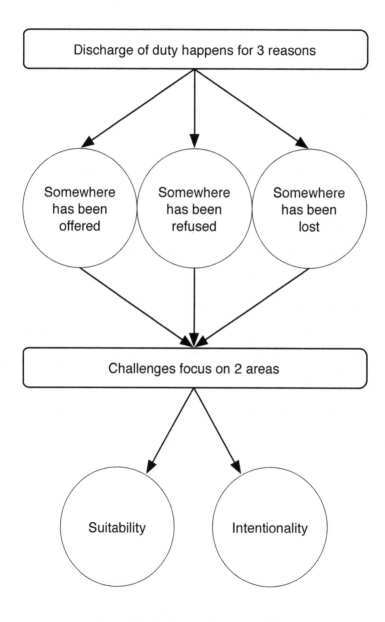

*Figure 18: Challenging Discharge of Duty.*

Once a local authority has accepted a full housing duty, it must continue to provide accommodation for that person until that duty comes to an end. The duty can only end in specific circumstances and must be ended in the correct manner. These are set out in full in s193 of the 1996 Housing Act Part VII but are summarised below.

The full housing duty can only end with one of the following:

1. A Part 6 offer: i.e. an offer of social housing from the allocation scheme.

2. A PRSO offer: a relatively new power of discharge, which means an offer of a year long fixed term private sector tenancy. It's more of a postponement than a discharge.

3. Discharge due to a refusal of temporary accommodation post decision.

4. Discharge due to becoming homeless intentionally from temporary accommodation post decision.

5. Discharge due to abandonment of temporary accommodation post decision.

s193 has lots of subheadings and sub-sections but all means of discharge are really for just three reasons; somewhere has been offered (the first two above), somewhere has been refused (the third option above), or somewhere has been lost (the last two above).

Challenges to any discharge of duty post decision focus on just two areas: suitability (the first three above) and intentionality (the last two above) as well as the way any discharge has been carried out.

## How to Challenge

Any discharge of duty is challengeable by the standard s202 review procedure, just like a full s184 decision. All of the same criteria apply and you can request accommodation pending the outcome of the decision. The same time frame applies, though in practice, such reviews may be resolved much more quickly.

Any discharge of duty must first of all have been preceded by a full reasoned offer letter setting out consequences of refusing or losing the accommodation in question. Without this, any discharge of duty is doomed to fail at the first challenge, so make this the first aspect you check.

The local authority's decision must then be accompanied by a fully reasoned Discharge of Duty letter. If it is not, then the local authority cannot be said to have properly discharged their duty; how could any applicant exercise their right of review without a decision letter? If no letter has been issued, then challenge your local authority that they have not in fact discharged their duty and that the full housing duty is still live and your client should therefore be re-accommodated.

Both the initial offer letter and the discharge letter should be scrutinised to ensure that the local authority has applied the correct tests and carried out its duties in the correct manner, just as you would for a s184 decision letter.

The one exception to all of this is the s188 duty to accommodate (see overleaf), which runs until a decision letter is reached.

# Discharge of Interim Duty: A Myth

Another bit of myth dispelling. Any loss of temporary accommodation prior to a formal decision being made is known as the loss of s188 interim accommodation. It is a very commonly held belief that the local authority is entitled to discharge this duty just like the s193 duty. That is, if an applicant refuses an offer of s188 accommodation, is asked to leave or abandons such accommodation. However, this is not necessarily the case.

Local authority housing departments will even often have actual decision letters headed 's188 Discharge of Duty'. Unfortunately, there is no such duty 'discharge of s188 duty' in the Act. If your local housing authority are doing this, then they may be acting outside of the law.

The law states that the s188 duty continues until a decision is made. If your local authority tries to discharge its s188 duty, ask them for a copy of the particular section of the Housing Act which describe the discharge of s188 duty. As there is no such section it will be interesting to see what you are presented with.

One of the few homelessness cases around s188 accommodation is that of London Borough of Ealing ex p Surdonja (1998) which asked whether s188 accommodation must be suitable. It concluded that it should be, so one area of challenge for a refusal or loss of s188 accommodation is on the grounds of suitability. However, the main issue is whether s188 interim accommodation can be discharged at all. It doesn't look likely.

Politely request that the local authority continue to provide accommodation until a lawful discharge of duty is permitted. If they refuse, then challenge by way of Judicial Review. As before though, this should not be necessary more than once and even the first time, it should not have to go further than the initial pre-action paperwork once the local authority realise how the s188 duty works and doesn't work.

# Discharge of Duty: Part 6 or PRSO Offer

If your client has received a discharge of duty decision because they have been made an offer of accommodation under Part 6 from the allocations scheme, a Private Rented Sector Offer (PRSO) or of temporary accommodation, which they have turned down, then you are essentially looking at a suitability review. Lets look at each of these offers in turn.

# Discharge of Duty following a Part 6 Offer

## 1. Examine the Offer Letter

Challenges to Part 6 offers from an allocation scheme have two aspects. The first one focuses on the offer letter. It must contain the following:

A statement saying that the applicant can accept and request a review and the consequences of such OR that they can refuse and request a review and the consequences of such. If the letter does not contain this, then you have already won the challenge; the letter is unlawful from the outset.

The reason for this is that when a Part 6 offer of accommodation is made as a discharge of a Part 7 homelessness duty, the applicant has two options if refusing it.

A person can refuse it and refuse to move in and request a review of its suitability. In this case, if their review is upheld then they will be made another offer. If it is not then their temporary accommodation will be cancelled and they will need to find their own accommodation.

Alternatively, a person can refuse it but move in and request a review of its suitability. In this case, if their review is upheld, then they will be made another offer, but until then they can stay in this new property. If their review is not upheld, then they can still remain where they are, in their new tenancy.

It is clear which is the less risky option and how important it is that any person being offered accommodation is in receipt of the full facts before making a decision. But it is surprising how many local authority offer letters do not contain this relevant clause.

## 2. Use the Suitability Criteria

The second aspect is a straightforward suitability review.

In considering whether or not a particular property is suitable, the local authority is required to consider all of the following 6 points (listed in bold for clarity):

**1. Part 9 and 10 of the Housing Act 1985** covering Slum Clearance and Overcrowding.

**2. Parts 1 to 4 of the Housing Act 2004.** Covering: housing conditions, licensing of houses in multiple occupation, selective licensing of other residential accommodation and additional control provisions in relation to residential accommodation.

In reality, neither of the above two criteria are likely to apply to any Part 6 offers of accommodation though overcrowding could be relevant to temporary accommodation offered as a short term remedy.

**3. Affordability criteria as specified by the Homelessness (Suitability of Accommodation Order 1996 (SI1996 no 3204).** This lists matters that local authorities must take into account in regard to the affordability of the accommodation in question. A copy is in your cloud file.

This statutory instrument requires the local authority to consider the following

(a) the financial resources available to that person, including, but not limited to:

- salary, fees and other remuneration;

- social security benefits;

- payments due under a court order for the making of periodical payments to a spouse or a former spouse, or to, or for the benefit of, a child;

- payments of child support maintenance due under the Child Support Act 1991

- contributions to the costs in respect of the accommodation which are or were made or which might reasonably be expected to be, or have been, made by other members of his household;

- pensions
- financial assistance towards the costs in respect of the accommodation, including loans, provided by a local authority, voluntary organisation or other body;
- benefits derived from a policy of insurance;
- savings and other capital sums;

(b) the costs in respect of the accommodation, including, but not limited to:

- payments of, or by way of, rent;
- payments in respect of a licence or permission to occupy the accommodation;
- mortgage costs;
- payments of, or by way of, service charges;
- mooring charges payable for a houseboat;
- where the accommodation is a caravan or a mobile home, payments in respect of the site on which it stands;
- the amount of council tax payable in respect of the accommodation;
- payments by way of deposit or security in respect of the accommodation;
- payments required by an accommodation agency;

(c) payments which that person is required to make under a court order for the making of periodical payments to a spouse or a former spouse, or to, or for the benefit of, a child and payments of child support maintenance required to be made under the Child Support Act 1991;

(d) that person's other reasonable living expenses.

**4. The suitability of the property for a person's medical and physical needs.**

**5. Whether a person may be at risk of violence or harassment at a property.**

**6. The physical location of the property offered.**

A suitability review can seem to be quite complicated but in reality, almost all cases concern themselves with the final three points. However, with the nature of social housing changing, along with changes to welfare benefits, the affordability even of social housing, is increasingly becoming a genuine concern.

# Discharge of Duty following a Private Rented Sector Offer (PRSO)

This is a new method of discharging the full homelessness duty with an offer of a private sector tenancy. Such offers come with a lengthy list of suitability criteria, which are contained in two documents in your cloud file:

1. Supplementary Guidance on the homelessness changes in the Localism Act 2011 and on the Homelessness (Suitability of Accommodation) (England) Order 2012.

2. The Homelessness (Suitability of Accommodation) (England) Order 2012. No. 2061.

PRSO's must be for a tenancy with a fixed term of at least one year without a break clause. Challenging such an offer covers two areas of suitability; location and condition.

## 1. Location.
This includes the earlier test of location as part of a suitability assessment, but it also goes further in looking at offers of accommodation outside of the local authority's district.

- Accommodation offered outside the local authority's district is not suitable if similar accommodation is available within the district, unless there is a justifiable reason for offering accommodation outside the district.

- Local Authorities should consider any disruption the location of an offer of accommodation would have on a household's employment, caring responsibilities or education.

- Established links with schools, doctors, social workers or other key services and support should be able to be maintained.

- In assessing the above, it is not necessary that such links should be broken to render the accommodation unsuitable. Issues of cost and time of travel to maintain such links and the impact of any loss of contact are all relevant.

- The nature of medical and other support facilities in the vicinity of the accommodation offered should be considered. This can include informal support from individuals, groups or organisations a person currently has links to.

- The existence of public transport links, local shops and other general facilities must be considered. Locations isolated from these would not be considered suitable.

## 2. Condition

- Properties must be considered suitable under s3 of the 2004 Housing Act, covering the Health and Safety Ratings System. Overcrowding and space standards of suitability must be complied with. The property must have been visited to check these aspects by either a local authority officer or a representative. Always check that this has been done.

- All electrical equipment provided in the property has been inspected and meets the requirements of regulations 5 and 7 of the Electrical Equipment (Safety) Regulations 1994. Request proof of this.

- Furniture and furnishings supplied must comply with the Furniture and Furnishings (Fire) (Safety) Regulations 1988 (as amended), and a fire risk assessment must have been carried out on any common parts of a building (for multi occupied buildings such as flats or HMO's). There must be a valid gas safety record (where applicable) and a record of the installation of carbon monoxide alarms.

- The building must have a valid energy performance certificate as required by the Energy Performance of Buildings (Certificates and Inspections) (England and Wales) Regulations 2007.

- If the building is a licensable HMO then it must be licensed or it will not be suitable.

- Authorities should satisfy themselves that landlords of accommodation secured under s 193(7F) are fit and proper persons to act in the capacity of a landlord. Local authorities are required to consider any convictions in relation to landlord and tenant law, fraud or other dishonesty, violence or drugs as well as any discrimination and/or sexual offences as set out in the legislation.

- The local authority should ensure that the landlord has provided to them a written tenancy agreement.

As you can see, the list for whether or not any accommodation offered as a PRSO is lengthy. Each of these is a ground for challenge and only one needs not to have been met in-order for the property to be unsuitable and any offer therefore invalid. The local authority must not just have taken each of these into account but must also be able to show that it has done so in relation to you or your client.

It is also worth bearing in mind that the making of a PRSO is a power and not a duty. If a local authority is offering them with a high frequency to those seeking to make applications check two things:

1. That the local authority has a policy around the use of PRSO's and is adhering to that policy. If it does not, then challenge and ask why, because the use of them may then be unlawful or discriminative.

2. Challenge the local authority on the grounds that it is operating a blanket policy, if it appears to be making PRSO offers to most applicants without due consideration to individual circumstances.

It is also worth bearing in mind that accepting a PRSO and requesting a review is a) the less risky solution and b) the most troublesome option for a local authority. They then risk the situation of a tenant newly signed up to a year long fixed term obligation in a property which a review has decided is unsuitable. If a tenant has to stay in unsuitable accommodation for a year, the question of compensation might be worth exploring. This is something which just hasn't been tested yet.

The other aspect to PRSO offers is that they aren't really a discharge of duty at all, despite the common perception of them (and their placement in the legislation). They are really just a postponement of the full housing duty because an applicant can reapply within 2 years and, as long as they are not homeless intentionally, priority need is not looked at (even if it has ceased to exist), local connection is not lost (even if they have been living outside of their council's area) and a full duty is immediately reinstated. This can be viewed as a very prudent 'banking' of a 'full housing duty', particularly if any priority need is likely to not last for the next two years.

Finally, who is to say what the housing market will be like in two year's time? There may be many cases where it is better to apply and deliberately seek to be offered a PRSO for these very reasons. In a few year's time, local councils may be regretting 'discharging' their duty to people under this power if such applicants come home to roost 'en masse'.

## Discharge of Duty following Refusal of Temporary Accommodation

When a local authority accepts a full duty towards a person they must offer them temporary accommodation. This is under s193 which is the next accommodation duty after the initial offer under s188. If the person refuses that offer then the local authority can discharge its duty, having fulfilled its responsibility to offer suitable temporary accommodation which is reasonable to occupy.

There are a number of ways to challenge such a discharge of duty.

## 1. Examine the offer letter
When making an offer of temporary accommodation post s184 decision, the local authority must provide the person with a letter stating the following:

1. The possible consequences of refusal or acceptance of the offer.
2. The applicant's right to request a review of the suitability of the accommodation.
3. That the authority are satisfied that the accommodation is suitable.

Ask your client for a copy of the offer of temporary accommodation letter. If they did not receive one then the local authority has acted unlawfully and the discharge of duty has no merit because the accommodation was not offered in the right way initially.

## 2. Examine the discharge of duty Letter
Following any refusal, the local authority must also notify in writing the applicant that they regard themselves as ceasing to be subject to the section 193(2) duty.

This must set out in full, just like a s184 decision letter, the reasons for the discharge of duty.

## 3. Examine the suitability of the offer
As above for the part 6 offer. Any accommodation offered, even if temporarily, must be suitable for the applicant and reasonable to occupy. Apply the same grounds as above.

Any failure in adhering to any of these clauses renders the offer and any subsequent discharge, invalid.

# Discharge of Duty if Homeless Intentionally from Temporary Accommodation
If a person is asked to leave temporary accommodation made available to them following a s184 decision then duty may be discharged on the basis that the person has become homeless

intentionally from the accommodation made available to them.

Local Authorities will only rarely carry out a full intentionality assessment of the person in order to reach this decision, but the criteria is exactly the same.

### 1. Examine the offer letter
Does it meet the criteria set out in the previous section?

### 2. Examine the discharge of duty letter
In addition to all of the criteria just discussed regarding the refusal of an offer, does it show that the local authority have carried out a correct assessment of intentionality in order to reach this discharge decision? They should be using the six point test looked at earlier.

### 3. Examine the accommodation
Did it meet all of the requisite suitability criteria? In this context, if you can show how it was not reasonable to occupy in the first place, then no intentionality discharge can be carried out.

If the answer to any of these questions is no then you are able to challenge, by way of a s202 review, the authority's decision. The lack of a full intentionality assessment is likely to be the most easily successful.

## Discharge of Duty due to Abandonment
A local authority will sometimes discharge its duty when it believes a person has abandoned temporary accommodation made available to them. If faced with such a situation, look at the following:

• Did the local authority give the person written guidance regarding any time spent away from any temporary accommodation? If not, the applicant can hardly be blamed for not knowing what they should have done.

• Were the person's belongings left in the property?

• Was a reasonable time frame given?

- What did the local authority do to confirm abandonment?

Treat this just as if you were dealing with a tenancy abandonment; look at who had keys, what were the general circumstances and intentions?

As before, always look at the offer letter, the discharge letter and the suitability of the accommodation itself as well, just as in the previous sections.

# 15. Principles of Administrative Law

Housing law is public or administrative law. This means that it is less concerned with the end result, but the process of how a decision was reached. The principles are there to guide that decision making process of a public body. They are very important to learn. They are what underpins not just homelessness legislation but case law. They are the grounds on which appeals are sought and are very useful to bring to bear at s202 review level as well. Make use of them in your challenges.

Below are ten important principles of administrative law relevant to homelessness:

1) The authority has wrongly interpreted the law or misdirected itself.

2) The authority has taken into account irrelevant considerations, or omitted to take account of relevant considerations.

3) The authority has reached a decision that no reasonable authority could have reached/has made a decision dishonestly.

4) The authority has failed to act in accordance with the principles of natural justice.

5) The authority had operated a 'blanket' policy.

6) The housing department must make its own decision and not merely rubber stamp the decision of another body/authority.

7) The authority should give a reasoned decision.

8) The decision must be based on the facts of the case.

10) The authority must consider using a power (even if it properly decided not to do so in a particular case.

# 16 Further Reading

The Homelessness Code of Guidance for Local Authorities. Now only available online, at:

*https://www.gov.uk/government/publications/homelessness-code-of-guidance-for-councils-july-2006*

Or bitly:

*http://bit.ly/1gUfmNv*

And its supplement (concerning intentionality and mortgage repossessions):

*https://www.gov.uk/government/uploads/system/uploads/attachment_data/file/7842/1304826.pdf*

*Via bitly:*

*http://bit.ly/1mnUJjq*

Homelessness and Allocations, by Andrew Arden QC, Emily Orme and Toby Vanhegan. This is the recommended guide to all aspects of homelessness legislation. Very easy to read and understand.

*http://bit.ly/M62jy9*

The Manual of Housing Law, by Andrew Arden QC & Andrew Dymond.

*http://bit.ly/1kNFFd8*

Housing Allocation and Homelessness, by Jan Luba.

*http://bit.ly/1nGytwB*

And your cloud files at:

*https://app.box.com/GetHousedDocuments*